MW00439956

Spirituality of Sport

BALANCING
Body and Soul

SUSAN SAINT SING

Susan Saint Sing

ST. ANTHONY MESSENGER PRESS
Cincinnati, Ohio

Cover and book design by Mark Sullivan

ISBN 0-86716-516-2
Copyright © 2004, Susan Saint Sing
All rights reserved.

Published by St. Anthony Messenger Press
www.AmericanCatholic.org
Printed in the U.S.A.
04 05 06 07 08 09 10 5 4 3 2 1

"Remember to remember God"

A saying I keep taped inside my front door...

CONTENTS

DEDICATION

This dedication cannot be to just one or two people. No one who is a team player ever achieves his or her goal alone. So many people help along the way. So many circumstances shape the experience and help glide the leaf that much farther down the stream toward the finish line that I wanted to take this moment, this time, to show and state my appreciation for the many who have helped this one person find her "one chance for greatness." (from the motion picture *Chariots of Fire*—"Seek your one chance for greatness and seize it.")

I wouldn't be writing these words without the help, gifts and encouragement of the following:

Dr. P. Prithvi Raj and Dr. Richard Greg, the two doctors whose gift of healing saw me through my days at the Pain Control Center in Cincinnati. Francis MacNutt whose gift of spiritual healing bolstered my spirit when it seemed I just couldn't go on at times. Murray Bodo, Franciscan poet, writer, friend; Taddeaus Taylor, Australian Franciscan; and John Schreck, Franciscan brother and Xavier University crew boatman—your friendship and stories kept me centered and focused in the long hours.

The friends and formative people of my youth, Coach Dick Rimple, Music Director Clyde Scott, our insurance man Mr. Gearing, Walter Fowler, Stella, Beth, Pam, Betsy, David, Mrs. Clark, Mrs. Minier, Dean Henry, Mr. Dobler—you believed in me.

My friends and professors at Penn State, Doris, Elaine, John, Gus, Linda, Father Joe, and Archabbot Leopold, Betz Hanley, Dr. Lucas, Dr. Kretchmar, Dr. Woodruff, Dr. Eckhardt, Rashanna Moss, Pete Holub, Dori Sunday and Reagan, William Buckley, Bill Joyce, Jackie Esposito, Dr. Secor—you all helped me see the greater horizons, trek toward them and reach them.

My rowing crews who I am very proud of and whose many names I cannot possibly list, but I will try—Nate Bishop, Pat O'Dunne, Kelly Weaver, Huge One, Kenny, Hallie, Marissa Weber, Rachel Morgan, Justin, Tess, Tessa, Lobos, "Bird man," Howard, Shawn, Katherine, Jon Stine, Stephanie Bachman, Mike Welsh, John, David Ahlert, Gary Wahoff, Shawn Cox, JoAnna, Meagan, Betsy Evans, Al Grandmaison, Josh, Tina Belotti, Neil, Kris V. and "T"—"Very Good." To the women of the Kent School's third eight who were "Athletes of the Week" stroked by Samantha Hunter. To Scott Cunningham, Pic, Shadle, Greg, Tony, Adam, Megan, my would-be women's four at Lynn, and to the hundreds of others, including Coaches

Eric Houston, Mark McQuinney, John Biddle—hearing you all call me "coach" means everything.

My friends, Debo, Bertie, Michael and Marilyn Wilson, Michael Sipkoski, Don Aldo, Damian, Kelly, Ingrid, Ted, John, Kenny, Clete, Bob Ernst, Jan Harvil, Sandy, Jeff Bauer, Tom Hartke, Tim Garry, Jr., and Tim Garry, Sr. —you will never know the impact your lives have made on me.

To Molly, Sam, Isha, Squirt, Pippy and Tex who were literally *always* at my side through nights of pain—your devotion as creatures toward me makes my devotion as a creature toward my Creator pale. And to Dr. Grady and Dr. Graves—thank you.

I have probably forgotten people and please forgive me if you read this and do not see your name—you are not far from my heart.

Finally, my family, my mom and dad, my aunts and uncles—thank you for teaching me so that I could teach others. As I once said to Uncle Bud (who asked me how I sailed ten thousand ocean miles over four years), "I'm just carrying on what you all taught me on our fishing trips to Canada and out on Lake Erie when I was a kid." He replied, "Then carry on."

All I can say is, "I'll try."

FOREWORD

It is Thanksgiving Day, thirty years after I ran in the Berwick Marathon. Once I came in second, once I came in third. I don't remember which year I did what, I only remember being determined to run. I had been sick for two weeks before the one race and my parents didn't want me to enter, but I did. I had to. I loved to run. I lined up, cocky, confident and ran—even with my fever pounding in my head my feet pounded out the miles.

At the top of Market Street I turned and headed back into town. I remember the boulevard being filled with people, as I ran—as these youngsters do today—to the corner of Second and Market in the "Run for the Diamonds." This race is some ninety years old and hundreds of people flood the tiny little mountain town to race for a diamond watch. And they take it very seriously. Today the helicopter overhead is competing with the Channel 16 TV news crew, trying to record Mr. Rimple as he announces the local runners in the throng as they run by.

I remember starting out all right, running on automatic pilot, letting the miles slip by. Then I remember feeling like I was not attached to the road, I remember seeing the finish line, staring at the finish line still three quarters of a mile away and then, suddenly hitting the pavement, hard. I lay there a few seconds and I remember my inner world screaming at my body—get up! *Get up!* And in my stupor of exhaustion, fever and sweat surrounded by snowflakes and gray skies—like today—I heard footsteps. I knew I had to get up, officials were running to my aid, my friends and even strangers were yelling, "Don't touch her! Don't disqualify her! She can do it!" I got to my hands and knees and I looked down the asphalt of Market Street hill; thirty years later I can still feel its cold, flat, road-smooth texture beneath my fingers and palms, as I pushed up, off of it like a swimmer launching from a platform. All I remember was hearing the breathing and the footsteps behind me. But they stayed *behind* me and I didn't lose second place.

The pictures of me in the newspapers weren't flattering for a high-school twirler, but the toughness showed. And it is my prayer for these young runners here today and all those who have run since me and will run, that when they fall in life they can go inside to that deeper place, beyond consciousness and will themselves forward and keep whatever is pursuing them to fail, in check.

This is a great gift, a communion, a holiness of spirit and flesh or spirit transcending flesh that is not easily honed or explained. It is a discipline, like faith, that can only be witnessed to and lived by, the truth of its measure only found in the direst circumstances. And it is my prayer for you that you form that place within yourself, pray for it, put the "miles" needed into it every day—and I pray to God that I never lose mine, that I don't have to visit it too often, and that it never fails me, or I it.

I believe in this place because I've had to go there, live there, visit it in times when my body was failing. I make no pretense that it is a pleasant place to be, but I can assure you that the greatness found there is the strength of the Other that meets you.

CHAPTER ONE

Arête

There is no substitute for experience. There is no substitute for finding out for one's own self, for the personal revelation, for knowing firsthand.

When I run, that happens. The body and the spirit become one. Running becomes prayer and praise and applause for me and my Creator. When I run, I am filled with confidence and the faith that word contains. I can face unanswerable questions, certain that there are answers.

The religious experience, you see, is too important to be confined to church. It must be available to me every moment. When it is absent I am, in that sense, no longer living. I am existing. I am on life supports, outside of me, like a patient in a coma. I am unconscious, unaware of what being human means. One way to come out of that coma is to be a runner.

—George Sheehan

T O UNDERSTAND MY IDEA for writing this book called *The Spirituality of Sport: Balancing Body and Soul,* you must go on a journey with me. As with all journeys, at times there will be periods of learning and knowledge, at other times periods of historical backdrop, reflection—like stopping to watch a sunset. Other parts of the journey may seem like an uphill climb—difficult, stretching your understanding and acceptance, yet part of the terrain to be covered.

I look at the body as soul. This is to say that while on earth the two can be experienced and expressed as a wondrous union—oneness. The body of an athlete in particular is a temple constructed to worship, to achieve perfection. My understanding of the soul is similar—an integral part of my every breath of life which seeks to be perfect, seeks to return to the place of its making—God. The soul in our mortal state is with us in our body, and we feel its urgings. The body is our mortal being. The two are one, a communion that can achieve greatness.

An athlete has a heightened awareness of both. Having been an elite athlete, I can assure you that the body's temple is at times driven on the fumes of the soul alone—that is to say, there is a place in exertion where an athlete goes beyond normal metabolism and kicks into an afterburner of something other—something spiritual—found or emerging from a sacredness within. I believe this link, this core, this pool within that athletes dip into in times of extreme competition is a reflection of the very essence of the energy of God.

This energy has many faces, many expressions. Anyone who has seen a marathoner nearing the end of the race knows, sees, a "terrible" expression of exertion—a body suffering to achieve a goal. R. Tait McKenzie, famed Canadian sculptor of athletes, framed the stages of this exhaustion in a series of bronze masks called *Agony*. There are other expressions, as when we have been pacified by the gentle drifting of a sailboat steered on the wind. In that gentleness an energy we seek moves us. And at different times in our lives the energy changes its expression. As children we enjoy running and climbing and playing on swings—as adults we turn this play into more serious sport. A child doesn't typically engage in play to the point of extreme exhaustion as a marathoner does. The child plays because it is fun. I believe the child at play is in touch with the purest essence of the energy of God. And as adults in our more sophisticated states and layers of "life" pressed upon us we seek to compete, as the highest level of play. An athlete typically plays to win something—a medal, glory, money. A child will play just for the fun of it and is not driven as we adults are.

I believe it is this impetus to play that we experience as children that is the truest, closest expression of the energy which an adult later experiences as the mortar of body and soul. Both are building blocks in the expression of the other. Both seek to unify to build something strong and impenetrable, a communion where the two together become greater than the individual parts. An athlete in touch with an inner core of peace and strength has an advantage by tapping into the energy of the universe—the playfulness of God.

What makes up this mortar in the communion between body and soul is perhaps a mystery. How we as humans react to and respond to God's presence in and around us has been interpreted in many ways. In my background, growing up as a Roman Catholic, I don't remember being taught that God was instrumental to my being a good athlete. I was to think about, pray to, and worship God, and partake in the sacraments and the Mass. Yet to invoke God's strength in a race, a race against someone else, seemed as if I was calling on God in order to be uncharitable and beat another. What if they were praying to beat me? Were we putting God in a quandary?

But I always sensed God was with me when I ran—as if the more I sweated and pounded my feet into the pavement, the closer God seemed. My running course in Berwick, Pennsylvania, took me down to the foot of Market Street, over the bridge toward Nescopeck and Wapwallopen. The bridge swayed as I crossed, the sterile river below ruined by coal acid from turn-of-the-century mining. The area was vivid with history, having played an important part in the Civil War as a Union stronghold for black powder manufacturing.

Near Berwick there are eel walls in the Susquehanna River, man-made mounds of river rock piled to interrupt the eels' natural feeding progress up and down the current, channeling the eels toward the walls' tips. Vertically, the stones were stacked wide at the base, narrower at the top, sturdy enough to walk out on, forming etched chevrons in the surface flow. These walls, untended since the 1800s, still stretch along the riverbed for miles. Horizontally, each wall extends hundreds of yards from the shore, south to the middle of the river and back north to the opposite shore.

The Susquehanna is the largest river in the state of Pennsylvania and here on the North Fork it was a good half-mile wide with sporadic islands. The river was quite shallow; on a hot July afternoon you could walk out to the center island along the top of one of the walls and never get your knees wet. At least I didn't.

The Vs formed by the eel walls survived from season to season, generation to generation. They once belonged to families and the rights for the eels collected at the walls were zealously guarded and jealously protected—sometimes by guns if necessary. When I saw these Vs, as I did daily on my training runs, I imagined them to be some colossal victory symbol from Zeus, coded in the river's surface just for me; such was the effect of my head in the clouds.

Ancient Olympia and Greek gods were my constant imaginings. Blame it on my parents who had taken me to the Carnegie Museum in Pittsburgh where I saw the sculpture hall with its life-size wax castings of Ancient Greece's Oracle of Delphi. Ever since seeing the museum pieces from Ancient Greece I wanted to be one of them.

Understanding the Greek philosophy of play and sport is important to our modern world. The Olympic games, a worldwide phenomenon that is older than our Catholic faith, has been celebrated and respected by both ancient and modern societies. There are few social gatherings that can claim such a high berth. And even though Greek culture is the foundation of Western thought and culture, the Olympic games are celebrated and recognized by Eastern cultures also. We owe our sports heritage here in the U.S. largely to the Greeks and to the English. This phenomenon of sport and culture was initially a religious celebration to the god Zeus. Athletes were like gods, champions rewarded with a year's wages and animals, wine and olive oil—enough to make a poor person rich.

It is not so different today. An Olympic gold medal will secure, in most cases, financial independence for the winner via endorsements, speaking engagements—the proverbial box of Wheaties. The bodies of Greek statues of athletes look very similar to today's bodies, the spirit and soul of those athletes is probably not much different—driving for success, fame, winning, self-improvement. We don't play our games to honor Zeus anymore but we have our gods. Some of the gods we have created are our national honor, the almighty dollar and our own egos, to name just a few.

Are Olympians special? I would have to say yes—that somehow they are blessed. Call it luck, call it fate—there are those that for whatever reason make it through a very special gate and become Olympians, while countless thousands might have similar talent and skill but due to injury, or circumstance, lack of means, a bad day, do not get to don an Olympic uniform. Olympians are special.

An Olympic spirit is a special quality that emanates from great souls—in Olympians and non-Olympians alike. The spiritual quality of an Olympic effort is the essence of this book on body and soul.

The Greek ideal of *arête*—symbolized by an equilateral triangle whose sides are body, mind and spirit—is the foundation of a balanced human being, the three balanced strengths of the consummate individual. When I was growing up it became my goal. I ran. I tried to feel the power of spirit. I imagined the equilateral triangle was carved in my river, *arête* and eel walls, flowing majestically right in front of my house, life giving, flowing into me.

I can only express it by saying that the more I ran, mile after mile, the closer I felt to something inside me that I experienced as happiness, relaxation, recreation of my mind and body—in short, a positive energy in my mind. Theologian Josef Pieper, in *Leisure: The Basis of Culture*, likens what I have felt to a biblical text, "the divine wisdom is always at play, playing through the whole world."

In my understanding, play is an invitation passing back and forth between the energy of God and the energy here in this world's creation, mirroring the last memories of the last perfect human state and union with the Creator—the Garden of Eden. The concept of play, in my understanding and experience of it, is like a return to Eden, a memory pushing through layers of consciousness and breaking surface like a wave on a beach. And when it does, we, like children, toe the sand in glee for a moment, and then it is gone. The response, the communion, returned and exchanged with and to the Creator until the next time. We have within our power the will to engage or refuse that Presence; and in the refusal, we lapse into the shadow of our darker nature.

One person who understood and joined into this positive energy of creation was Francis of Assisi, as when, for example, he picked up an imaginary violin and danced through the countryside of Umbria. In the harsh environment of thirteenth-century Italy, there were such movements as the Albigensian heresy, just one of many superstitions that labeled the body as essentially bad and of the darkness; many were influenced by such perspectives. Francis' positive reaction and his response of impulsively dancing in God's spirit reminds me of King David dancing before the Lord in ancient biblical times, or the Shaker medleys and their heritage of dancing with glee in the spirit of the Lord.

Francis struggled with his frail body—at times he called it Brother Ass, thinking of it as a beast of burden and an obstacle to his longing, perhaps, to be totally free of the flesh in order to join his Heavenly Father. It was only at the end of his life that Francis, now carrying the wounds of the stigmata, embraced his own body and admitted to his followers that perhaps he had been too harsh after all, and that God had revealed to him that Brother Ass was really Brother Body.

To me this exemplifies the redemptive journey. We learn as we go, and sometimes it is an uphill fight. But the path is already laid out for us by those who have gone before; they experienced the same difficulties, wrestled with the same questions. Their discoveries can lead us if we choose to follow.

Early in his conversion Saint Francis danced before his friends and neighbors, and before the Lord, with the joy and playfulness of a child, as a creature free and reveling in the wondrous works of his God. He then struggled with the seriousness of God—how does a creature comprehend the Creator? And at the end of his life, Francis reconciled body and soul and redeemed his own mind, his spirit—back to the light burden of Christ, back to a childlike playfulness and lightness and certainty of heart—as evidenced in his Canticle of the Creatures.

Balancing body, mind and spirit gives you a strength like a triangle—the strongest building unit. If each side of the triangle is balanced and equal then you have achieved great strength. Like the ancient Greeks, you achieve the heightened state of *arête*—a state of grace and excellence. Linking the mind-body-spirit trinity could be the energy of the divine wisdom playing through the world. This energy at play in the world I see as goodness, and I experience as a vital part of the presence of God. In this energy we experience God around us and we experience and respond to God's strength and power and joy in us and through us. It reminds me of a Celtic prayer from A.D. 300 or 400—"God within me, God without, how can I ever be in doubt. I am the sower and the sown, God's self unfolding and God's own."

This image of being the sower and the sown is our own being to which we gleefully, playfully and appropriately respond from a childlike stance that is simultaneously adult. That is to say, as children we play and as adults we tap into that playfulness and find an inner well of beauty, peace and strength. A spring of clear, cool, life-sustaining water—it can be different for each of us and its origin is God.

That said, though everyone can play, not everyone is an athlete. Not everyone has competed in a sport, not everyone's body functions as it once did due to age, injury, circumstance. You may not want to be an athlete—this book is not just about sports, it is about the communion of effort, the conjunction of two worlds. If you believe in the world of the spiritual and you believe in the world of the flesh and you believe that the two are mysteriously in unison through Christ's redemption, then you don't have to be an athlete to find meaning in these words.

The fluid nature of water is integral to understanding our journey. There is a flow, a soft edge to the meaning of "body, mind, spirit" that will often flow into the holistic "body and soul" metaphor. Allow your understanding to go beyond the individual words, to see body/spirit/mind/soul—as a whole concept, reduced for convenience to body and soul.

Body and soul is a metaphor acknowledging the spiritual, just as "blood, sweat and tears" is a metaphor for the purely mortal. When we experience the union and force of both these worlds—flesh and spirit—we glimpse the miracle of the resurrection, we know, for an instant what Christ felt when he opened his eyes on that slab in the tomb—fully human yet fully God—the surge for a second of exuberance, jubilation, joy! To be alive, to breathe and sense every cell of the body responding, *living*. I believe that we experience the experiences of God in our own lives in our own circumstances, to our own limits of tolerance and understanding as part of God's plan for creation to be transformed. The experience of body and soul is but one sequence, one path in that plan for us to live as Christ lived and to glorify God as he glorified God, for the ultimate purpose of being God to one another. With him, in him, through him, we return to the ground of our making—the energy that is God, that is life, in this world and the next.

Body and soul is as much a state of mind, a whisper of perfection on the wind, as it is a physical, emotional state. It is about not just having a great spirit, but *being* a great spirit. Body and soul is the lamination of the death and resurrection of Christ—fully human and fully God. Obviously we don't walk around in this awareness every minute of every day—just as Christ rose only one morning. But I believe it is an archetypal experience in the collective unconscious of this world that is here with us and at times is tapped into and we see it and recognize it, like love, because it is part of our own template. It is a glimmer of hope, a peek at what we are to be whether running in the Olympic games, strapped to a hospital bed, or waiting to pick up the kids from school. We are called to be great in all things.

These primordial ripples are around us because God is always around us and therefore the experiences of God are always around us, *for* us. We are an integral part of the experiences of God because we were with God before we were born—we were with him on the cross and in the tomb and in the manger. That is why we shudder at times, and lift our head slightly in awareness, like a gallant horse who stops and sniffs the wind, sensing something, recognizing something so powerful that the horse stops in full stride to be enveloped by it. Such is the experience of body and soul—it is the recognition of God's creation. It is that moment of mystery when the shroud of our human state *is* with our divine state—and we know it. We experience the truth of our faith—that God exists. And we know that it is all true, from that moment forward we can never be the same.

And that is the rush of energy and sheer joy and super-humanness that we feel and experience and know. To *know* that we are, without a doubt, more than just body is gift. To know that we are body and soul is to live in the hope and the fact of resurrection. Body and soul is the human experience of the primordial forest, close and damp around us with mystery and intrigue and primal animal-like consciousness and heightened awareness—like that of the horse—joined, amplified and at the same time tempered and honed by the reins of the divine. Body and soul is the pinnacle of human goodness—fully human and fully godlike. An athlete, for example, who cheats and wins the race is not experiencing body and soul—perhaps only body and body. No, body and soul is the flesh made whole, if only for a moment where our efforts are recognized as beyond human.

In his work on mythology, Joseph Campbell once said that when we as mortals experience heaven here on earth, then that *is* heaven. To know and to be one with the divine nature and to *know* that that is what we are experiencing and witnessing to the point that it makes an indelible etching on our existence is the privilege of achieving a balance of body and soul. And to choose to strive for that unity is the directional quality of this text, as a handbook, a manual, for those who want to try or for those who seek to understand something they have seen or want to see, want to accomplish or at least align, tune their world to, be they coaches, athletes, administrators, parents, pastors, spectators—to understand, to teach, and to strive for the balance of body and soul.

It is a journey. God knows I have gotten lost many times already along the way. But of those paths of which I am certain—I hope to share my insights.

CHAPTER TWO

The Well Within

Reach down
farther still
and bring forth
within yourself
living water,
whose life
will nourish
and refresh you
and whose birth
spills forth the seed
of God.

—from "Pilgrim in Assisi" by Susan Saint Sing

FOR ME, ALL THE YEARS of pounding miles through the heat on July afternoons, past the close stench of Mud Swamp, up the long, make-or-break hill of Bower's farm, plodding alone, listening only to my feet on the blacktop, an occasional red-winged blackbird or curious groundhog monitoring my way, created a depth and belief in myself that brought me eventually to the World Championships. I didn't know at the time what I was making, or what was being made inside me, other than the lactic acid which was causing my lungs to beg me to stop. But I know now, that those years of training, discipline, physical toughening built a reservoir inside me, a well that I still don't know the depths of.

As an adult I went on to spend nearly two years of my life in Assisi, the home of Saint Francis. The people I met there, the mountains, the Umbrian plain, Brother Sun, the Franciscans and, I think, Francis himself, cuddled me in the olive trees and mountain air, amid pealing church bells and medieval revelry to a place inside of myself, perhaps an archetypal place of healing inside all of us that calls to us in a faint yet indelible voice to come and lie down by the still waters of peace—to heal, to drink.

There isn't much water in that arid environment, but there are springs and wells channeled throughout the pink granite alleyways. Spouts stick out from walls from gargoyle heads. Open air laundries and ancient Roman watering troughs lie reflecting the seasons of Brother Sun and Sister Moon. The well in the courtyard of San Damiano's rests demurely, waiting for anyone to lower the bucket and drink.

Though these images of water, granite, and lead are tangible—I do believe that drawing life from an inner spiritual spring is ancient within us. It is our job and our duty to really tap into it, tell others about it, teach young people how to recognize it, to respect the hard work it is, to not be lazy about seeking it, to tear at the opportunities to seize it when it is at hand, and to sit back in near worship when we see it being drunk from. Great athletes drink from it. They find a way, a channel to draw it forth and let it trickle inside. It is the inner well that marathoners sip, so they don't hit the wall. The wide receiver who is running at full tilt and catches the perfectly thrown game-winning touchdown pass passed the cup in the huddle before.

Ritual is one of the symbols of religion, so are transformation, union and sacrifice. Sport has all of these, yet I don't want to term it a religion as some authors have; but I will go so far as to say that when we are involved in sport, we involve our body and soul in what can be a religious experience. To a Catholic, it is pretty easy to find solace in Christ crucified and feel the beating heart of the Christian athlete motif. To a Native American like Jim Thorpe, perhaps running made him feel part of the greater creation, wisdom. When you go deeply inside yourself, as you do in prayer in the quiet hush of a church, you seek something of solace, strength—a place where nothing else exists but you and the Other and you are, if only for a moment, totally taken into and with the Other. In this sense, when body and soul face each other—the body totally spent and searching with the soul, its only partner with which to find more—a religious experience is at hand. Body meets soul, soul enlivens body, body and soul experience a miniature Calvary, tomb and resurrection—and if the mind is paying attention, a remnant of cloth is solidly present, lying there as witness to the communion of creature needing and meeting Creator.

I am not a theologian or a psychologist, but I have spent the better part of my life—and I am nearly fifty now— guiding athletes to this precipice, this teetering edge of performance, bringing people to that place, that moment where they seek to go. Why? I believe they do it, we do it, to see what we are made of—meaning to see if there is anything *more*, anything other than flesh and sweat and blood. We do it to see if there is a soul looking at us in the extreme fumes of exhaustion. As in a near death experience, we go in a controlled fashion into these realms to see, to explore the depths of ourselves, begging of the Other. Like a pilgrimage, a cleansing, a retreat, we emerge more human, more alive, more aware.

For many, the physical experience, the "high" is all they seek, for them it is enough. But I think that is sterile. To me, it is as if they walk (or run) right past the tomb of Christ and never bother to look inside, never seek to enter the kiva, never enter the sweat lodge to wrestle with their demons. To me, they perhaps haven't gone far enough. True religion begins when the body cries out through its soul in recognition and *relief*—the veil of self-protection and self-importance rent—because it sees, knows (hence the biblical term "witness") the presence of the Other who was right there next to them all the time anyway. True religion begins when we finally "get it."

The ritual of running or any other sport—getting up at 5:00 A.M. for crew practice, donning certain clothes, stretching, doing the same things over and over makes it a ritualistic activity. Tennis players hit hundreds of balls to practice placing their serve near the lines—finding the edge. Golf is no exception, die-hard golfers wear lucky shirts, one glove, only certain colors; they test the wind, hone clubs to specific degrees. Runners, basketball players (remember Pistol Pete Maravich's lucky socks?) all have rituals that they *believe* in. Why? Because the ritual worked somehow for them before—they won a game, or did their best. Participating in sports is a testing ground. We are tested. Our bodies and our beliefs are tested. We are put (or put ourselves) in the cauldron to be made into gold, literally gold medals—the precious purification of biblical rituals.

We test ourselves in sports. The isolation of the competitor, though voluntary, can take one to the extremes of the desert experience—exhausted, dehydrated, at times clawing one's way face down after collapsing on a track or falling on a snowy mountain slope. The symbolic parallels between ritualistic sport testing and faith are so close, so obvious that even the ancients used them, as did Saint Paul, as metaphors of one another.

Of course, we could easily see sports simply as competition; some of it for noble causes—as in the proverbial "race well run." Or who can forget Olympic hockey goalie Jim Craig draped in the American flag staring into the stands asking where his father was seated after the 1980 Miracle on Ice? Other games are scored for less noble purposes, such as running animals to the death on tracks or taking risks beyond even heroic measures to prove oneself, many of which have ended in death or severe injury. Aspects of sport are sometimes enough to send us all into our closets, basements and garages to pack up, sell off, throw out old water-ski tow lines, dad's favorite second baseman's glove, the broken skateboard and the new, prized golf ball driving net, used twice. And I think we would, particularly as we get older and the sport complex fees get steeper, were it not for that elusive integral coming together, becoming as one of body and soul that calls us to the ski hills, the driving ranges.

A friend, Doris Aruda, summed up this fusion for me in a succinct statement after she won the national karate tournament with grace, speed, dexterity, lethal threat: control to within a fraction of an inch by an interior realm and plane of discipline practiced as surely as any combination kick, "We are not angels. We are *meant* to be body and soul." This unity cannot be fractured; it is how we were created to be. It was from this center of body and soul that she brought her total self to the match. It is toward this center within that I orient these explorations. It is to this fusion—this lamination—that I bow. When an athlete becomes so self-aware, a communion, a transformation begins.

Perhaps I should take Doris's advice and not attempt to dissect the experience of body and soul. But in my thirty years of standing on track fields, ski slopes and beside rowing waters, I have heard countless stories. Stories that should be told, and are as relevant now as when spoken between uprights of football fields or carved into the ice. The loud speakers have blared out the names who have sought it. Parents and family have waited, cheered, suffered, celebrated. This tapestry hanging just beyond, yet encompassing the athletes: the invisible, indelible, intangible but thoroughly perceivable dimension, is the real trophy and memorabilia worthy of collection.

I don't know any athlete who has reached the top, or tried for the top, without it. Athletes are simultaneously supported by and exasperated by it, lovers encourage it yet are jealous of it, teammates and opponents, teachers and coaches drive them to the brink of collapse for it. Trainers both soothe wounds and prepare knees, muscles, minds for battle in it, fans are for and against it, rivals fuel camaraderie (till next year!) over it—all uttering a combination of well wishes and caution, discontentment and encouragement, prescription and challenge, curses and prayer, thanksgiving in both pain and glory. Such embroilment drives deep inside to the very sinews of existence, beyond physical to the metaphysical, fueling a constant internal to external traverse through it. Such antithesis and synthesis, and the avenues toward its making, are worthy of record.

But what is *it*? What is it that unites body and soul? What makes "the body electric?" What is it that we *know* when something greater is there, out there on the field or in the gym? Perhaps you have experienced a moment "frozen in time" when time seemingly stands still because something great has happened. I experienced this when Pete Rose hit his record-breaking base hit—it was as if the universe stood still, time stopped. The same thing happened when Carl Lewis in 1996 jumped in Atlanta to a record Olympic gold. I knew I was witnessing a milestone and I was *part of it*. I think what we are responding to, either as a participant or as an informed witness, is the experience of grace.

A human effort has been graced by God. We, in our creaturehood, having come from the Creator, and being still
enlivened by the energy and spirit of the Creature—inher-
ently respond to this communion—even if only in wide-
eyed, awestruck wonder. Something intangible electrified
the action, the effort, and this resonates with a template
within us. The template is the memory or recognition of
godliness.

When a human being is elevated for a moment to the
heights of the gods, the audience wants to know. The fans
want to be there. Nobody wants to miss Carl Lewis, on his
last attempt, long jump to a gold medal. At Mass, you
don't want to miss the consecration of the host because
that is the moment of grace, the miracle of Christ's effort
on the cross redeemed for our sake. Jesus took away our
sin, gave us back the blessing of peace and play. It is a wonderful experience in worship when this blessing of peace
and play descends on a room or church and laughter or
dance or holy slumber spontaneously breaks out. Our
spirits are renewed in the presence of God. Our spirits are
renewed when we are in the presence of God's grace;
beauty, form and function all pointing to one end—the
higher moment when body and soul, flesh and spirit meld
and are no longer in opposition but are one unity—one
harmony.

One of the greatest exhibitions I have ever seen of play, I saw one spring afternoon in Millheim, Pennsylvania on Route 45. I had driven out to this valley dozens of times, on my way over to Bucknell University from Penn State. This valley is considered a historic route, the Pennsylvania "Orange" Tour, known for its rolling hills, cornfields, villages of log cabins still used today, Amish farms, carriages and clotheslines flying black pants, blue shirts and white aprons in the wind. I'd seen countless Amish families working in the fields, and their life, while intriguing and demanding respect, always struck me as hard; maybe harder than need be, certainly anachronistic, with farms next to theirs boasting direct TV discs on the barns.

I'd seen great testimonies to their belief in simplicity—like the father and young boy I saw one day, the boy barefoot, both in the black suspendered pants, blue shirts, each driving teams of plow horses, father in front, son in the rear, matched sets of chestnut behemoths dutifully obeying the reins, even the light, yet uncertain, tugs of the tiny lad. I'd seen a woman, twice, late in the afternoon, riding a horse-drawn cultivator of some sort, drawn by four horses, plowing a twenty-foot swath of ruts up a sloping grade. Dust rose thirty feet behind her, yet she drove the horses on, unconcerned, in a light blue smock tied with a white apron and topped with her white cap. These people work hard.

I'd seen open buggies, more a carriage than the boxed styles you usually see, with young men driving one tall horse for Sunday afternoon's "going-courtin' " ritual that has been done for centuries along the same lanes in the same cold air and crisp light. The faces handsome and robust, the eyes unwavering, meet mine sometimes, and the look is one of childlike beauty, peace—and the flowers on the seat tell a tale of the simple joy that awaits a young woman somewhere in the hollows. These images are common in my mind's eye.

But there was one day, shortly after their school let out, that has left an indelible impression of joy and happiness and mischief that was refreshing, surprising and delightful. There on the back of one of the box-like carriages, in a line of six carriages, was a tall strapping blond Amish boy with a huge smile, beaming white teeth, his long black coat swaying from side to side, his hat pushed back on his head and his hands clutched securely to the bobbing back of the carriage rails as he *roller-bladed* home! I started laughing out loud in my own car, with no one to hear except me and God, and I tossed him a thumbs up out my window which he caught in the corner of his eye, faced me just a second as I whizzed by and he positively beamed in glee and delight. The kid was probably sixteen years old and the thrill of roller-blading elevated his spirit *and* mine. His sincere and absolute engagement with the fun of his task—and the impish look as if he knew he might be crossing new ground for his people—seemed to please him inwardly, and he seemed happy that I had noticed and that I knew and would not forget as the carriages became small dots in the rear view mirror and I drove on.

Witnessing pure play on a roadside in central Pennsylvania, or on a lined, measured field, reveals and reinforces to the mind that harmony is possible. Harmony is as near as the well-executed effort. In a world such as ours, where commercial jetliners crash into towers lining crowded city streets, and beautiful princesses are killed in high-speed paparazzi chases, simple farmscapes and carriages filled with teenagers are necessary to remind one that life is beautiful, and that harmony is welcome.

The Greeks, in their pursuit of excellence, strove for beauty as a combination of grace, elegance, learning, poise, goodness. To the ancients one could not be beautiful and do ugly acts. And I must say, looking at that Amish boy roller-blading and his sister gawking out of the oval carriage opening, laughing with him, was beautiful. They were innocent, handsomely featured, physically strong and upright with a carriage that was polished to a high shine and a horse that pranced in his harness. This was an exceptional vision of harmony in the best sense. Theirs was not a life of drudgery at all, and here was the proof. Their life was much more joyous and balanced than mine, as I sped away, in my usual hurried rush to get somewhere else and do perfunctorily whatever it was that was scheduled for me that hour. I was not in harmony at all, yet in my new car, nice clothes, grand education—one would think I should be. Here were two worlds meeting and mine was the one out of balance, not theirs. The boy was in his world, and even his balance on his wheels—grounded with the carriage, grounded to the earth—was symbolic. The edges of two worlds were juxtaposed, one in harmony, one not.

Harmony is a tool that must be handled and used as a craftsman uses a fine plane to straighten and join opposing edges of wood. Planing and joining opposing layers and "edges" in our daily lives, so that our daily existence doesn't always feel rough and full of splinters, is really the task that we are all trying to master in one way or another, isn't it? And learning to use the tools we have to build a harmony through practice and trial and error, is part of the pursuit of an excellent life, a life with the by-product of harmony, peacefulness, relaxation—like the satisfaction we find in relaxation, hobbies, play. Harmony is the product of a well-played game.

Games establish artificial balance, for a time, within which real life is left "out there" somewhere. The game preempts the outside chaos and for awhile we are engaged in the game; we create rules that are based on order and balance that allow us to see one another as equals, give no one an advantage, strive to maintain fairness. And while we are participating, we experience fun, joy and a sense of well-being—not a bad idea. Games and sport teach us of boundaries, skill, fun, hard work, fairness. They can of course run amuck and turn into stampedes of raging fans or players who are outside of the beauty of the moment, but that end is not what we strive for.

To strive to push one's body in a channeled effort, while seeking to dive into the recesses of the soul for fortitude, courage, strength, honor is a marvelous dichotomy for a human to try and bring together. Mark McWhinney, National Scholastic Champion Crew Coach at the Kent School, puts it this way, "Nobody rises to low expectations." In other words we should strive for transformation. If we can learn to call upon the graces around us while in the heated battle of an all-out athletic effort, we are excelling, we become leaders, we are coupling the flesh with the spirit and creating a sacrament. We are sacrificing (ask triathletes whether they are sacrificing themselves) offering *ourselves* for the greater good, the outcome, the finish line, the goalposts, the judges' box—we have broken the barrier of fear, gone through the limit of our own comprehension of self and learned creaturehood and gratitude and humility.

This is the moment of grace, of knowing with indelible recognition the fruit of faith, that something greater does exist, and for a moment you were part of it—and its memory holds you in wonder and worship, and you never forget—as when Christ's robes brushed through the crowd and the person who was seeking his healing grace received it. This moment Michelangelo frescoed into the ceiling of the Sistine Chapel—the touch of God, unity and extension—the harmony of having come from something greater with the assurance of being able to return—the assurance that we are not alone or bereft. The assurance that we can run a marathon, the marathon of everyday life, and when we stagger across the line there *is* someone, something benevolent, waiting.

CHAPTER THREE

Why Should You Row a Boat Race?

I never heard anyone profess indifference to a boat race. Why should you row a boat race? Why endure long months of pain in preparation for a fierce half-hour that will leave you all but dead? Does anyone ask the question? Is there anyone who would not go through all the costs, and more, for the moment when anguish breaks into triumph—or even for the glory of having nobly lost? Is life less than a boat race? If man will give all the blood in his body to win the one, will he not spend the might of his soul to prevail in the other?

—Oliver Wendell Holmes, Jr., on receiving the Doctorate of Laws, Yale University Commencement, June 30, 1886

SOME THIRTY YEARS AGO, after injuring my neck and back in a gymnastics exercise, a huge depression set in. I suppose it was inevitable. I was not in balance. I lost touch with the well within. I stumbled on the journey. My life was tilted, leaning, like a top ready to fall off its center. I had the image many times of a wagon carrying the baggage of my life, rumbling out of control down a bumpy road, and precious things were falling out—like my physical ability: the ability to run, for instance, and the ability to go through a day without pain. In fact, at the Pain Control Center I attended, patients were required to go to counseling so long as they were getting treatment. They figured if you were sick enough to be there, it had to be compromising your life in other ways too. The need to regain balance and not be blown over to a side of life, clinging to darkness and depression, appealed to me. I always believed in the Greek idea of balance and *arête*. It is an integral component of the inner athlete and relates directly to the mystical. As the three muses are to the arts, the three principles of *arête*—body, mind and spirit—are to athletics. Living the concept of the *arête* of ancient Greece helps athletes, helps athletics.

I did not realize at the time, that this entire incident of the injury and being at Penn State and my father's dying, would tie together in a glorious plan, that still to this day, I marvel at. Because of the above circumstances, the tragedy opened doors that I think would otherwise have remained forever closed. One such door was a friendship made with a man, our campus minister at Penn State, Father Leopold, who later became Benedictine Archabbot Leopold. This man introduced me to a deeper spirituality. He became my confessor and a lifelong friend until his death in 1991. We discussed my going to Italy, alone, to the town of Saint Francis, where I could rest and where I thought I would be healed. I went.

I found a way—sipping from a cup that was literally held at times for me by doctors, physical therapists, friends, family, my Catholic beliefs—to burrow my way out from underneath the dump truck full of pain and depression that buried me. I spent nearly two years in Assisi, working for room and board, writing and singing about Saint Francis, no longer capable of being very physical, I became a spiritual athlete. When I returned to the United States, I had no idea where I was headed, I only knew that I had been healed somehow inside and I was ready and balanced again. Like Francis, I had crawled into my subterranean dungeon and up into the caves of Mt. Subasio. I had seen my lepers waiting on hospital gurneys as I waited for yet another doctor, another test, another procedure.

I was working as a freelance writer, which did not demand much of my physically impaired body and was asked to cover the Collegiate National Rowing Championships for the Sunday Magazine Edition of *The Cincinnati Enquirer*. My big break! When I went to the lake for a 6:00 A.M. practice and talked to a coach about the article, he piped up, "Well, you're kind of small, and our coxswain is sick today, so if you want a crew story, why don't you get in that eight over there and cox it for us." I was mesmerized from the first stroke. This was it, finally, an outlet, a way to be athletic and use my competitiveness and years of athletic prowess without using my body.

I got so wrapped up in the steering, the movement of the shell beneath me, the serenity of the lake (minus the exuberant coach with the twenty-watt megaphone yelling things like, "Okay guys, take it up two in two. Let's pick it up! Swing! Swing!" that sounded like a tango or waltz instruction) that I forgot to take any pictures for the article I was supposed to write. Lucky for me. When I sheepishly explained this back at the dock, the coach beamed and replied, "I guess that means you'll have to come back tomorrow."

Tomorrow and the next day and the day after that, I was there. I was hooked. I knew I had made the connection and crossed the barrier between sport and no sport, pain and being able to compete anyway, use of my athletic prowess without exerting my body, a means to plug in all my years of competitive drive and savvy. I could use my mind and all its watermanship skill and knowledge, my athletic drive and my deep desire to be an athlete again. Being able to compete again lifted tons of heaviness.

I was a cox. I was whole, my mind, body—though altered—and soul were clicking! I could write and make money selling articles, I could compete and I could at least be physically active and vital to a race—without pulling one stroke. Doors opened. Opportunities arose and before

I realized who I was coxing for, Olympians and world record holders were in the seats in front of me, names heralded in sports circles, names like: Chris Penny (*True Blue*), John Terwilliger (*The Shell Game*), Wieslav Kujda (Olympian), Harry Graves (Royal Henley Record Holder) and Kris Karssians (Junior World Champion). I could now write not from the vicarious sideline, but from the seat.

I began to "feel" the rowing. I was part of it—it was underneath my seat. Each stroke a slice in the surface of the water disappearing in the morning mist. A launch, a coach, eight rowers and a coxswain—ten people in the morning mist. These ten people are in one effort, to propel the boat forward—fast. Rowers seek the elusive moment of swing when eight are as one and the boat lifts slightly and seemingly flies. The pulling becomes almost effortless and speed picks us excitedly. All wasted effort and vibration has been shed—it is a magic moment—it gives rowers a glimpse of what unity can be and do. And they love it!

I don't know any other such movement in sport that elicits such a reaction from equipment and crew. Authors write about it, coaches look for it, rowers pull for it—and when it happens it is more than energy and movement. And once it is experienced you have a crew—they have bonded—and everything is compared to that one elusive piece, regatta when they had achieved swing.

Regatta is not a word on the tongue of most Midwesterners or youngsters who grow up in coal towns. I tended to associate it with gatherings held on the manicured banks of yacht clubs. Modeled somewhat on the Royal Henley Regatta in England, *the* most upper-crust boat race in the world, my first race was the spectacle of the 1986 Cincinnati Regatta. Rivaling the Frisbee throwers and folks with picnic baskets, "official" regatta accoutrements abounded. On shore, starched, white, double-breasted suits were *de rigueur* for the ladies. For the men, modest university jackets, pocketed with three-tiered, gold-embossed emblems of past collegiate honors won, plated buttons with school insignias and simulated nautical rope piping on the seams, were set off with a crew tie of crossed oars or club colors.

On the water and in the crew area, dress was at a minimum. Sleek, close fitting togs and tank tops give unrestricted movement for the competitors racing hundredths of seconds apart, trying to gain every advantage of "walking through" an opponent like a giant centipede. I coxed in that regatta and I kept coxing till I found myself competing at the U.S. National Championships. I became the head coach of Xavier University men's and women's crews, Program Director of one of five U.S. National Training Centers for Rowing, and in 1993 a Manager to the U.S. National Team at the World Championships in Prague, the Czech Republic.

In all those years of waiting in hospital waiting rooms, those tedious physical therapy exercises, the daily compliance to restrictions and the tiny incremental steps of progress nearly indiscernible that you live for I learned patience and respect for the seemingly mundane and natural processes essential to most achievement. So when I asked Hartmut Buschbacher, Women's Olympic Sweep coach, what I could do for him as manager at the Worlds he replied, "You make these rowers feel at home (we had a very young inexperienced team that hadn't traveled abroad much, certainly not to a former Soviet-bloc country) and keep them fed with a consistent American diet for three weeks, and we will win medals." Sounded simple enough, not what I anticipated for world-class racing strategy, but I was a creature of process by this time, so I started to implement his request.

I didn't entirely grasp the scope of his words said nonchalantly three months prior to the Worlds on the banks of Eagle Creek Reservoir in Indianapolis at the U.S.

Nationals, until I arrived at the hotel in Racice and began what was to be numerous conversations and a lasting friendship with Jidka (pronounced *YID-ka*), the owner. Comfort and good diet seemed like oxymorons to Czechs in 1993. I showed up at the hotel out of uniform to sit down in the restaurant with my translator, unnoticed, unannounced. Thinking I was ordering sensibly, I asked for the most expensive meal on the menu, a meat dish with gravy and potatoes, and I asked for a plate of mixed vegetables on the side.

Slowly and deliberately the waiter served a plate of greasy, indiscernible meat (intended, I was told, to be eaten with beer [!] not the Coke I had ordered) and a plate of steamed red cabbage. I asked the waiter to take it back and give me a plate of mixed vegetables, stressing mixed; they returned with a plate of green steamed cabbage. I then asked the translator to try one last time, and he stressed fresh and the waiter returned with white steamed cabbage! So I understood at that moment what we were up against: red, green, and white cabbage was the limited extent of their mixed vegetables. So began a week's transformation to turn the kitchen, dining room, staff and available food into an American-style cafeteria.

I had worked in the *pensione* Casa Papa Giovanni in Assisi,

Italy; and I knew how to set up a kitchen—prices, ordering, quantity and good old finagling. Since we were being
housed with the Brits, the New Zealanders and the Hong
Kong delegation, I started making phone calls to these
managers telling them what to be prepared for and setting
up a barter scheme: the Brits would bring a truckload of
apples and fresh fruit if we would share the 2,431 boxes of
Kellogg's we were getting from Battle Creek. The New
Zealanders couldn't be expected to send much but did
inform us that they had found kiwis in Vienna the previous year. So they supplied information and savvy. The
Hong Kong delegation, consisting of only one rower, the
coach and his wife, agreed to eat, drink and watch whatever
the rest of us wanted, so at least they offered congeniality!

Once we had converted the kitchen into a walk-through
cafeteria with assorted lean, meatless and poultry dishes,
we set up a means of turning an upstairs meeting room
into the theater, and twice a week I drove forty-two miles
round trip into downtown Prague to pick up videos in
English—and even managed to select a variety of videos
to suit all the tastes of the team members, coaches, managers, doctors and trainers.

On a three meal a day rotating schedule shuffling 146
team members through a forty-two seat dining room with

a practice and competition schedule that ran from 5:50 A.M. till 7:00 P.M. seven days a week for a month, we managed to keep a flow of trainers, elevators, theater, food, coaching meetings, hotel staff, quiet areas, lobby patrol (for uncredentialed people looking to steal or for some unauthorized reason trying to get into the hotel) despite the physical limitations of the building.

All of these seemingly mundane concerns proved vital to the comfort and ease of everyday living and function yet to the inexperienced, they may seem superfluous and extraneous; they were the launch pad to the actual racing and all the myriad complications of boats, oars, transportation, uniforming, injuries, rules, schedules, etc., that led down the race course and to the medals stand. And win medals we did.

The entire U.S. contingent came in second to Germany, and we won more medals than any previous U.S. team. Time spent at the competition venue is only a fraction of the day, and keeping the athletes' minds occupied and uncluttered from everyday worries kept the athletes relaxed, and with some luck the entire unit rolled along through the days and weeks retaining its competitive edge.

After the hundreds of hours of preparation and thousands of details attended to, we reached finals week. Across the vista of water, boats, ceremony, weather and flags, a coach friend walked up to me, and rested his hand on my shoulder. I think he sensed my fatigue from working to a point of distraction, and said, "Susan, take it all in. This is the *world championships*. Take the afternoon off; there are some team members who want to go to Terazin (the site of a concentration camp eight miles away that had had a predominantly Christian internment). Why don't you take them?"

I wondered at his suggestion as I strode to the van to bring it around to the front of the hotel where I was to meet my charges for the day, at what type of a day off it would be.

On the drive over, I began to get an insight into myself and these other complicated creatures all around me called athletes and coaches. I thought, as we drove through the countryside of the Czech Republic, that here were athletes of the highest physical caliber, bodies honed to near perfection, going to a place that would remind them of the body in its most socially cursed form—burning in an oven. It was this single request, to go to Terazin, that provided the germinal idea for this book. That a coach at the Worlds thought it was a good idea; that the athletes wanted to go; that I was there accompanying them—these synchronicities I find important. The respect these athletes gave to these fallen victims in a far off land moved me deeply. Not one took any pictures, not one really talked; we walked respectfully in a hushed stroll taking it all in.

These young American athletes who would soon be racing for the world title were showing medal qualities. They were the living embodiment of *arête*, balance—superbly sculpted bodies with soul overflowing in compassion and concern. I was proud of them!

No one mentioned religion at all, but the twenty-foot high obelisk, the crucifix in the cemetery, with the Star of David on billboards all around the exterior walls, set a distinctive backdrop. A profound, tangible Presence in the van was unmistakable. The Greeks scraped the very sweat from the bodies of the Olympians and sold it, considering it sacred—I was beginning to understand why.

The spirit that moves one to contemplate and appreciate the spectrum of existence, strives to elevate existence. This thinking is *not* necessarily religious, but it is spiritual. Athletics can embrace a religious background or not, and being a non-religious athlete does not diminish the spiritual aspect of sport. Recognizing the spiritual is not a 1990s idea of Christians kneeling in end zones, being covered at thousands of dollars per television second! It is a tradition from over two thousand years ago when the first Olympic athletes honored Zeus to the present. Call it what you will, there is an inner core to great athletes that they draw from when they need it, and that they nurture, seek interaction with, and practice diving to the depths of.

The trip to Terazin was one such interior trip to the core. It was an interaction with symbolic meaning, focus, and in a way a terrible relaxation. In the interludes of silence I sensed that the young athletes I walked with were putting their experience of walking among these brick and stone witnesses to death into their own internal equations, their own cauldrons, sooner or later to yield something greater. This day trip certainly was the antithesis of the frivolity of stroking a sixty-foot-long, two-foot-wide, Kevlar boat 2,000 meters for the fastest time—World Championship or not. For this group of athletes, winning would *not* be everything two days from now in the finals; it would be but one more olive branch they could weave into the crown of their own personal triumph over whatever demons or darkness life would put upon them.

As we drove out of the prison walls that formed the physical camp of Terrazin that August afternoon, I related the story of Romuald "Ray" Thomas, Olympian, whom I'd met at a world coaching meet almost a decade before; his story still rings in my ears...

> I am now seventy-five years old. I rowed in the 1952 Olympic Games in Helsinki, Finland and in many, many World University Games. In 1951, as members of the Polish National Rowing Team, my partner Czeslaw Lorenc and I won the gold medal in Berlin at the World Games. Rowing has been a part of my life since I was in high school. In Poland we were chosen for sport by body build. Because I was tall, I think that is why I was selected to row—tall but strong. This strength I have always been grateful for. It seems that physical strength has helped me to survive when others were dying. In 1939 I helped defend my country against Russia and we had to march sometimes for thirty miles a day. I believe it was my strength from rowing and sport that made me stronger mentally and physically than others and so I could go on.

Fitness and this stamina saved my life when I was imprisoned during World War II. I would sit in my cell and in my mind rehearse every aspect, as technically as I could remember, of my rowing workouts. This helped pass the time of confinement and also to keep me alert mentally and to not give up—someday I would row again. I believe in body and mind and soul working together. I think mental strength is equal to physical strength. You must believe you are stronger—mental strength prepares you in case there is someone else physically stronger. I have never been beaten in twenty years by anyone in a single, pair or an eight. I have won over ten gold medals at the World Masters championships for veteran rowers.

I am not a religious person; I believe only in the natural evolution of things, but I believe the soul is the cohesion of body and mind. It is deeper than thought. Different from will. It is attitude and belief and character.

And echoing Ralph Waldo Emerson's essay *Self-Reliance*, Ray concluded, "You must believe in yourself no matter what, and then you will be all right." Ray Thomas's story reminds us that there is a heightened experience in competitive sport, that is different than play or exercise. I have experienced that even practicing for a big competition pumps up one's awareness, as if a mystical component comes to you and you achieve an elusive glimpse of success.

Sport, as touted in article after article, newscast after newscast, is frequently associated with some type of religious analogy—for instance, if tennis is a religion then Wimbledon is its shrine—not necessarily religion as in mainline Christianity, or Islam, or Judaism but a distinct spiritual, mystical base. And the essence of that spirit, that drive, that connection to the higher being, or higher self, or higher state of achievement is part of the striving any athlete seeks. It is what coaches yearn to pull out of an individual or team to gain the cohesion to perform as a unit; one mind, one purpose: to seek and find the edge of a previous best and go beyond it.

I have seen only those athletes that are a composite of both body and soul successfully compete and be complemented by sports. Those who seem to suffer emotionally but compete, I have seen as being people who haven't successfully united the aspects of body and soul. They find no ultimate peace in the means, only the outcome is their goal. Great athletes—and perhaps here I should distinguish that I am referring to coaches and athletes alike in that term, learn to lose and learn through losing because any time two teams compete on a field of play, someone wins, someone loses. I don't think any self-respecting athlete can let go of a loss easily—a loss haunts all of us, but the ability to overcome adversity and loss without losing oneself in innumerable ways, is the soul of a true competitor.

The idea of *Balancing Body and Soul* came to me in Prague at the 1993 World Rowing Championships, and again after the final score of the Super Bowl when a small group of athletes from both teams knelt in prayer on worldwide TV. At thousands of dollars per second, it was televised! This focused for me something that rang true to my own experience: athletes' belief in and deriving strength and purpose from the spiritual—is an integral component of their lives.

Why should anyone row a boat race indeed?

CHAPTER FOUR

Finding the Edge

Sports flow outward into action from a deep natural impulse that is radically religious: an impulse of freedom, respect for ritual limits, a zest for symbolic meaning . . .
—Michael Novak, *The Joy of Sports*

THIS MORNING ON THE PLANE I looked out the window of the Northwest Airlines puddle-jumper I was taking from State College to Detroit over Lake Michigan, when the dawn, sandwiched between water and rain clouds, broke in layers of dark, light, dark.

The image was one of those indelible moments that take hold of you, because you recognize it somehow as something part of you, meant for you.

All my life I have been sensitive to the two domains, dark and light. I was a person, for whatever reason, destined to be aware of both. Perhaps that's why I started to run.

Maybe I ran to flee; I was always running to somewhere from somewhere, always in between those two worlds, clashing as they play out their scenarios, like hurdles on a track for me to have to run over. I'd imagine myself sometimes at full stride like the great Edwin Moses gliding over them, refusing to stumble hard onto the track. But sometimes I did catch a toe and hit a hurdle and stumble hard. This book, this journey is for all those who stumble. To all those whose athletic spirit drives them on, forward, washing them with stick-to-itiveness, courage in body and soul.

To the athletes that kneel in end zones and to the ones who have never left their porch rocker on a warm Sunday afternoon, to anyone who is immovable in the face of injustice and sin and whose experience of life, whether drawing the attention of millions of TV viewers, or breathing the long-distance runners' mantra, or nimbly shuffling rosary beads, the message is the same—dark and light exist, so what should we do? The path to and from the light is a narrow slit and it is my hope that these musings while perhaps not new, find a unique renewal and signal to your athlete within that "something is up." Something is happening right now that cannot be ignored. God is a goal as well as a constant presence.

Many athletes cannot leave their wheelchairs, some are

Olympic heroes, others have an Olympic spirit—but the spiritual athlete within (or however you want to term the desire, the spirit within that strains at the whispers on the wind)—will resonate to the layering of the mystical within us. All spirit competes with the mass, the matter around us. By their nature the two are different and incompatible insofar as texture and nature. Body is tangible; spirit is not—though the ripples of quiet force surrounding spirit move us as certain as the blades on a windmill turn in the wind. Anybody moved by spirit over the long haul is an athlete in my book. For the body is transient and eventually fails, but the spirit runs, keeps running on. Like Olympian Edwin Moses stepping over the high hurdles in the 400 meter—spirit goes on, leads on, carries you along a track, a path sometimes unseen, but felt and experienced.

Only the combination of body, soul and mind make the experience whole and real as only our living state allows us to perceive. For any spiritual athlete, the grace of communionized body, spirit and soul is fullness of life. Grace and faith synthesizing experience to Olympic heights of transcending beyond the mortal to the edges of the dark and light, where worlds and the solidness of seen edges in clouds tells us that one place is different from another.

These two worlds are the metaphysical and the everyday reality. These worlds are the edges between the four medieval elements—earth, air, fire and water. When water and earth meet there is an edge—like my dawn over Lake Michigan or the beach at our family cottage on Lake Erie. At the lake's edge we are drawn to drag our kayaks out over the beach onto the water. We are drawn to listen to the gentle lapping of waves. It speaks to us and we listen. We try to understand and in our still attentiveness it writes its wisdom on our souls.

Jung states that by distilling the experience of one's life, one affirms that the survival of our civilization may well depend upon closing the widening gulf between the conscious and unconscious aspects of the human psyche (Jung, *The Undiscovered Self*). He continues,

> I hope therefore as a psychiatrist, who in the course of a long life has devoted himself to the causes and consequences of psychic disorders, may be permitted to express his opinion, in all the modesty enjoined upon him as an individual, about the questions raised by the world situation today. I am neither spurred on by excessive optimism nor in love with

> high ideals, but am merely concerned
> with the fate of the individual human
> being—that infinitesimal unit on whom
> a world depends, and in whom, if we read
> the meaning of the Christian message
> aright, even God seeks his goal.

So what is the goal of sport? Is it winning? Is it money? Or is it to teach values and fairness and healthy diversion?

A sense of the metaphysical in sport, a beauty that must be there, is necessary for great sport to whisper to us about itself. This is the voice of the *arête* in the ancient Greek athletics—a pursuit and ideal to strive for, a balance of body and soul and mind and character, values, grace, perfection, grace in strength.

Of central importance is the acceptance of the above as a thing of beauty. The transfiguration, while at times violent, must be a thing of beauty—ethical, moral, artistic beauty. The transformation of Saint Francis when he meets the leper is that the leper is not repulsive but an object of beauty. As a coach this is very central to my understanding of perfection. Perfection of the human being in its ultimate realization of exertion and movement is to behold beauty of skill, composition, grace, strength, elegance, mental discipline and if we can couple that with a performance played or executed within the rules, so that there is no tainting of the presentation—there is beauty; one has witnessed a reflection of God's perfect will for an athlete, for flesh and blood to move within spirit in ultimate form.

I see sport as a communion, a sacramentality in several layers. Certainly effort is a communion singularly or as a group to become something greater than what was. And in this quest for transformation we participate in the liturgy. We are the liturgy in that we seek to lift up and elevate our broken selves in order to become something greater, or at least be accepted in union with something greater.

In sport, I see beautiful movement and beautiful body as living sculpture—classic Greek-like, a reflection of the resurrected being—the ultimate prayer—Calvary. As a coach, I feel I contribute to this universal prayer of humility. By being privileged to teach—and to teach from the background of knowing pain—reminds me daily and serves as my taskmaster to acknowledge and live by feeling my creaturehood. To elevate sport to a sacred place where one can go and use visualization techniques as I did while getting another MRI or while lying in yet another operating room, is grace. And to see the beauty of human form doing and executing skills at the level of completeness and complexity for which it was created is prayer and worship.

God can be experienced as the Master artist who extends Herculean levels of spirit into vessels that come—either by force, as in injury or by ordainment, or by birthright— as inheritors of the spirit of God, familiar enough and comfortable enough to play at the feet of their father Abba, as children and as heirs.

Seeing the beauty of God in the creation of bodies is not new. Being bipedal—with an ankle that bends and a flexible foot to balance our stride and make it smooth and quick—was a choice made by God. We are God's design. We are designed in a fashion that not only pleases God but also is a tribute to a higher being's intelligence and vision. God chose us to be of muscle and mass, with the ability to move in myriad ways. This same matter can lie still and sleep, or pose for a painting, come alive in reading of action in a book while sitting, unmoving in a chair. This body of matter of flesh of which we are made is an extraordinary material. Our senses can pick up the slightest increase in draft in a stuffy room when a window opens. We have strength and tenderness in the same muscles. We are dynamic creatures, not static non-moving blobs. It is my understanding that our creaturehood begins with this limiting "thing" of matter that we are. We are body, we have an orientation, we have a head that is up and feet that are down. We are para-spinal in that we have a left and a right side—sidedness. We take up a space and inside this space we have a soul that lives and abides.

Saint Francis called this space of Brother Body his cell, referring to a monastic—not a jail—cell entered into for the sake of prayer and worship, a sacred place. I truly believe that athletes understand this concept and practice it. They might not call it a cell but they do worship the space it takes up on the planet, the air it breathes while swimming a 500-meter sprint, the distance it can reach while fielding a fly ball. We are of a design that is most accentuated when executing physical feats of beauty.

I think that is why an ice skater defying gravity while effortlessly gliding through the air, landing and spinning, arms extended and slowly tucked in, blurring to a column of flesh that seems as if it is drawing into itself, mesmerizes us. The energy of the act, its beauty and grace delivers us, takes us with it momentarily to a higher level of existence, a place closer to God, a centralizing focus, culmination—like the elevation of the body of Christ in the host during Mass. Just by the act of lifting the bread up, not out or down, is a directional focus that is intended. The movement alone guides us if we let it.

Play is an archetype of goodness and joy, a cluster of energy mirroring the last memories of the perfect human state and union with God—the Garden of Eden. Play is a return to that, a memory pushing through layers of consciousness and breaking surface like a wave on a beach where we, like children, press our toes in the sand for a moment and then it is gone, to resurface later.

And I believe that every athlete, male or female, has to ask and struggle with these concepts before they can become true champions. Like the skater, this edge is the balance, is the space between the action between the body and soul of an athlete; it differentiates between who is an athlete and who is a jock. It is the pivotal step one takes toward being a champion. Let me give an example. I know an Olympic coach who has coached for a quarter century. This man has been hired and fired a few times due largely to "politics." However, his graciousness and his genius prevails and in Europe and in the U.S. people walk up to him and shake his hand and smile and sometimes even ask for his autograph. I have pointed this man out in the crowd to my athletes and tell them stories about him, incidents that I have personal knowledge of and I tell them, "There is a ten-time Olympic coach and an Olympic medal winner. It isn't the medals you win or lose, it is the ability after twenty-five years to walk around a regatta site and have people want to say hello, and reach out to shake your hand that makes you a great champion."

A champion is seen as someone greater than the event, greater than the skill. "Champion" is a quality, a value champions exude through every day of their life not just the one day they crossed the finish line first in the Olympic games. However, because they trained and sought and listened to the whispers on the wind in those lonely desperate areas of the river, or empty stadiums or rain drenched tracks—they took their walk with the mythical. They touched the gods of despair and courage inside themselves. And we who have not yet accomplished this—seek them. We seek to applaud them and study them and in our own way worship them. That is why we fill stadiums by the thousands on weekends—we want somehow to vicariously be part of them—the athletes, the champions, and take a small part of that "champion" quality for ourselves.

True champions usually have been given many gifts—they are usually strong, talented, skilled and have the opportunity, the means and the mental wherewithal to stick to a goal. And to those who have been given much—like the above—much is then expected. They should be the humblest, the most gracious, the most helpful to their teammates, in short, good people. These are the true heroes and champions for my money—male or female, old or young.

If we don't at least try to assimilate these values into sports and competition then we run the risk of shaping small groups of win-at-any cost, arrogant jocks. If sport does not help us transcend our base nature, then why play? Why spend hours and days and months and years drilling the wrong message into young people's minds? For a medal that costs three dollars? I don't want to be a part of that, and I have tried—not always succeeding mind you—but tried to make sports something more, to plant the seeds at least to pursue excellence—*arête*, the beauty of body and soul checking and counterbalancing one another, pulling the other to a higher, better place—and us with it.

I say these words to young people and to the readers of this text because winning and losing is only a 50/50 proposition. If you are a competitive athlete, every time you go on the field of play someone wins and someone loses. I have stressed this previously. It is only when you pursue excellence—whatever level that is for you or whatever goal that is for you—that you are always a winner. And if you pursue excellence as a competitor, as a student in training under a coach, as a gold medalist or as the one who crossed the line in last place, and you pursue the basic excellence of being a good person—then and only then are you on your way to being a champion.

Nothing upsets more than "cheap shots" taken at weaker opponents, arrogance over winning, anger and tantrums over a loss. Certainly if you win big it is appropriate and great to celebrate and whoop and holler! To feel God's delight inside urging you to feel glee and unabashed joy is fantastic! Go for it! But to learn to lose is also part of the challenge.

First, it is important to define and look at the definitions of what is ethical and what is moral; are they the same thing? Not really. Ethics comes from the Greek term *ethos*, which means that what is right and what is wrong and can mean surprisingly different things to different people in sport. For example, some of the basic sport issues such as winning can be looked at from several different sides. Should winning and losing be a central focus in competition? Do zero-sum games teach children better than regular sports? What about driving up the score? If a person is coached to win, does the end score matter, so long as he or she wins? Do athletes play well if they foul in order to get the ball back in basketball? Is a deliberate foul cheating?

Are we teaching the wrong values when student athletes are encouraged to play for a school but don't graduate? These are all challenging questions.

When I was in high school we had a priest who asked our entire parish—during Mass!—to pray for Notre Dame football during the fall and Villanova basketball during the winter. I remember even then, at the age of fourteen or so, wondering why we were praying for these schools, which were in other states, during Mass. I figured the priest had an inside connection and knew that God must be a Villanova basketball fan instead of a Georgetown Hoya fan. I remember wondering why God would want to visit Philadelphia for a game instead of Washington, D.C. And we only ever were asked to pray for them to win. So I presumed God didn't like losing, and I vividly remember deciding to throw in a few elbows in basketball and smack a few field hockey sticks on opponents shins to be sure to do my part to win. I didn't see this as cheating; I saw it as not losing.

It wasn't until I was in college that a coach straightened me out. Seeing me bullying my way through a field hockey line, she asked me to step over to the sidelines, and without even looking at me (continuing to watch the action on the field) said, "I don't know where you came from, but here we win because we are *athletes* who are more skilled and more intelligent than other players, not jocks who push and injure others in order to score." I started thinking about that statement from this impeccably dressed Englishwoman who was coaching field hockey without ever raising her voice and dressed in boiled wool suits and stockings and heels, who was also the only coach, male or female, to win two NCAA national championships in different sports in the same year—an impressive pedigree. And even though I was in my high school hall of fame for field hockey and other sports, she benched me, and made it perfectly clear that I had a lot to learn before I would play on her team. Right then and there I decided to emulate her.

Thirty years later, I am now a coach at the same school and tell my athletes her words at the beginning of every season. Because I coach at a public institution, I cannot gather the crew around me to pray before an event. But personally when I was an athlete, and now as a coach, I have always prayed before every season and every practice and every meet. I pray for safety and for me to think and see clearly, and for my athletes to do their best.

If there is one thing that I believe has served me well and a quality that I see in the best of other coaches—it is integrity. You cannot cheat and win and gain the respect of others. That may sound simple and old-fashioned, but in sports winning is the object (although there are zero-sum games with the idea that everyone wins). Playing to win, while teaching people excellence, is the greatest gift anyone can receive. Teaching athletes to be their best, and to *do* their very best is the secret to winning. I had a teacher at Penn State once say, "Winning is only a 50/50 proposition; on any given day on a field of play someone wins and someone loses, but if you play your very best and you compete to be excellent, then you never lose, you are always a winner." I keep this saying in front of my desk. Striving for excellence in character, in judgment and in performance makes you a winner. Tom Landry, legendary coach of the Dallas Cowboys, once said something akin to—the secret to winning is learning to lose without losing your dignity. In other words, if goodness keeps you, your team, your program, on a path of excellence—not to be deterred by winning or losing, then winning takes care of itself.

Having said all of that, of course it is nice to win, and many jobs and contracts and places on a team are governed by the nature of competition on a winning record. And I think it is important to accept that parameter. I would rather try to win by pursuit of excellence and lose a contract, than cheat to win to keep a job. Any athlete or official that practices shortcuts to excellence, of which cheating is one, is never really a winner.

Ethically, the judgments one makes to fight, punch, cheat, make a call to favor one team, yell belittling remarks from the stands, or have fans so maniacal that they tear a stadium apart and trample people or beat up an opposing player on the way to the bus are disgraceful and give all of sports a black eye. As Catholics and Christians, I believe we should not be yelling, "kill 'em!" from the stands. I personally do not believe we should run up a score if we are securely in charge of a contest. Winning and losing are the byproducts of competition. The goal is to compete and then, as a result of the competition, a win, tie or loss results. There are various philosophies in sports such as zero-sum games (no scoring, everyone wins) and running up the score (winning by a large margin) that need to be understood in order to ethically and morally coach, participate, officiate or attend sporting events. These considerations are the essence of body and soul, to participate in fair play and old-fashioned sporting conduct. The very word *sporting* means to challenge fairly, as in the British phrase, "That's very sporting of you." Sportsmanship should entail respect; respect for the opponent, respect for the game, respect for yourself. If you respect those three you are always a winner.

Zero-sum games have their place from time to time and can even be used by highly competitive teams or individuals to vary a practice or scrimmage. Schoolteachers use these types of activities to teach the values of participation and activity—valid goals. But the notion of driving up a score, as is frequently done to secure a playoff berth (home team site advantage is frequently chosen by the amount of season points scored), is a highly questionable tactic, despite the notion that since we play to win, the margin of winning is irrelevant.

As tempting as the argument for running up the score may seem, most teams who have been beaten by a large margin feel a sense of humiliation and a pejorative sense of having taken a beating, not just being beaten. I personally didn't mind losing, necessarily, so long as we played our best. However, when the opposing team trampled us, it left a foul taste in my mouth. It is that sense of "foulness" that I hope *Balancing Body and Soul* addresses and clarifies. As persons who love sport and love to exercise their bodies, we should become champions of common sense, character, order and fair play. Sometimes the real champions finish *last*, as in the Olympic marathon in the late seventies when the final runner was hours behind the pack and still kept walking on wobbly legs, covered in dirt, near collapse but refusing to be helped or eliminated; he never gave up and finished the race finally crossing the finish line tape in the darkness when all the fans had gone home.

Like an athlete in training for the long haul, the marathon, the 5K row, the triathlon, body and soul become tools to use—means to a well deep inside to draw from—to find God and ourselves in.

CHAPTER FIVE

Heroes

(Un)Answered Prayer
He asked for strength that he might achieve;
He was made weak that he might obey.
He asked for health that he might do greater things;
He was given infirmity that he might do better things.
He asked for riches that he might be happy;
He was given poverty that he might be wise.
He asked for power that he might have the praise of men;
He was given weakness that he might feel the need of God.
He asked for all things that he might enjoy life;
He was given life that he might enjoy all things.
He has received nothing that he asked for, all that he hoped for.
His prayer is answered. He is most blessed.
—written in the inside of the chapel door at South Kent
School used with permission of the Dean of Boys, Chris
Allsop, Olympian

WHEN MY FATHER HAD his stroke, I skied faster that winter and ran harder and more often, than I ever had in my life. As I look back now, this was the time when I was given my first opportunity to suckle humility. My body alone had always made me feel better. But this time I could not train myself out of the sickening grief. I couldn't outrun it or out ski it. It had me.

It is only now, that I've begun to put the pieces together—to see, to feel, the experience of our creaturehood. Once we understand this, our role, our position vis-à-vis the Creator, everything else pretty much falls into place. We are created. We are mortal. Somewhere in those years of his dying and my injury, mortality hit me in the face.

Greek gods and perfectly balanced *arête* triangles of equilibrium seemed foolish and frivolous. My triangle, my hope to elevate the center point of a flat line to an apex, had been squelched irretrievably, I thought. I became more introverted. Who was out there? What was out there? Was there a benevolent God?

It took me years to answer that: I was given the knowledge not because I was special or graced, but because I was going to need it.

Once you experience the soul within you and its spiritual orientation acting as a guide for the body's course, you can't ignore it. You don't have to believe it, in the sense of having faith, because it does not require your faith in it to exist. God, in the soul within the body, is. If ever there was a total immersion into the present moment, it was Carl Lewis on his last jump of his Olympic career, in front of millions of people worldwide, striking the footplate and soaring to a gold-medal twenty-three feet. It took less than thirty seconds. Every sinew of his body and every sinew of everyone watching were unified into a gasp and then a roar as the stadium exploded into cheers. I was there in Atlanta for that moment, I was seated not more than fifty yards from him when he made that jump. Carl Lewis went into himself that night; and body and soul delivered.

Perhaps that is the greatness of it, the breakthrough when body and soul are equal and a Herculean task is accomplished by someone who was—a few seconds earlier—just a mortal. For in our current state outside of the Garden of Eden, outside of the perfect will of God, inside this existence on earth in the permissive will of God, our body, at least in our perception, is greater than our soul—because we see the soul as within. However, in an instance such as great love, or a great physical feat—the soul perhaps, equals the boundaries of the physical body, perhaps even spills out in love—and extraordinary feats are accomplished and recognized as being great because of this dual nature of the body—redeemed momentarily, reflecting the essence of its godliness, acts like a god—superhuman.

One such person is the story of Professor Emeritus, John Lucas—Olympic historian. This man was one of my undergraduate teachers at Penn State—a man I both revered and feared. This Boston-bred professor strode into class each morning and said, expecting a proper answer, "Good Morning, Class." And for some reason, our post 1960s irreverent class all answered, "Good Morning, Dr. Lucas."

It struck me that this man wore a three-piece suit to teach American and Olympic sports history class. We were a class of football players, varsity field hockey players and basic jocks. We didn't know it, but we were being transformed.

It began with understanding that sports were more than tossing or hitting a ball. Sport had a history, an ancient history going back to the Greeks, and that our American sporting history came to us via the Greeks to the Romans to the Middle Ages into the English schoolyard and upon our shores at Plymouth Rock. And this remarkable, staunch and stuffy New Englander was categorically walking our minds through cockfights, Spaulding and baseball, Neismith and basketball. In the middle of this immersion bath, my father died suddenly and I left school abruptly, placing notes in my professors' mailboxes (before the ease of e-mailing them), but I had somehow put his note in the box below, not above, the name John Lucas.

When I returned to school two weeks later, I had missed the midterm. I was still anxious and a bit blown away from the funeral and all the travel (I had packed up my mom from her Florida home and then made arrangements to fly her and my father's body back to Pennsylvania for the funeral). It was all a lot to handle for a twenty-year-old.

My dad's body somehow didn't make the plane when we

transferred planes in Baltimore and while we flew on, he—detained in a large snowstorm that blanketed the east coast in the late afternoon of the day we took off—rode to his final resting place in the belly of a Greyhound Bus. I thought, even at the time, that this was a particularly entertaining circumstance, something my father was getting a laugh out of.

When he finally got there, nearly late for his own funeral we buried him in Erie, Pennsylvania on January 12 in the middle of a snowstorm ourselves. I will never forget that day of standing by the grave with a winter storm swirling through the makeshift vents of the tent. I did not cry; I only stared at the snowflakes—trying to be one of them, anything but feel the pain of having lost him. The snowflakes were frolicking and floating, a part of the cold scene but comfortable in it. They were beautiful and small in their crystal tenuousness, not hard and wooden like the box resting on the brass holders, which seemed so incongruous with the earth. I never cried, and I spoke to almost no one.

Back at school, I had to face the backlog of tests, work and responsibilities. When I walked into Dr. Lucas's office—on the list of professors I had to see—I stood waiting inside the door, several feet in front of his desk in White

Building, waiting for him to lift his head and beckon me closer in acknowledgment. When he did, after several uncomfortable moments, I said, "Dr. Lucas, I need to reschedule my midterm" and before I could finish he stood up and glared at me with, "Well, I suppose by now you have gotten all the answers from your classmates and I will have to make up a special new test just for you. Where *were* you anyway?"

At this point, I realized to my horror that he did not get my note.

"*Well?*" he asked again, closer to me and louder.

"I was at my father's funeral," I managed to say softly more out of fright than sorrow.

He paused, I remember, turned on his heel, walked back behind a large wooden desk that was very boxy and that concealed all that was behind it, and he sat down with a heaviness I had not seen in him, and I remember noting it. He motioned, without a word, for me to sit down in the leather, worn chair that faced the desk. I sat.

He put his hands to his face for a second, I watched him sigh, as now I was totally taken with his movements and responses as he had gotten my attention. All I could think as my heart pounded was, "Was he going to flunk me?"

Then he spoke, without looking up, still apparently studying his hands and the top of his desk, "My God" he said in a hush, "Forgive me. I am so very sorry."

And it was that exchange, fear, yelling, miscommunication, reverence that cemented a relationship that would last the next thirty years and to this day. We had somehow crossed some threshold of acquaintanceship and professor/student relating that landed us smack in the realm of truth and understanding, equal footing, where our souls recognized one another seemingly for the first time.

And, as he got up from his desk to walk me to the door he gently asked, "Please join my wife and me for dinner this Friday, if you haven't any plans. I'll give you the address after class tomorrow."

And there it was. An invitation to eat dinner with the Official Modern Olympic Games Historian of North America, John Lucas. A remarkable man whose own personal Olympic story has been spotlighted in *Sports Illustrated*. It began in 1952. He was a 1500-meter runner who came in third in the Olympic trials—only the first two made the team. He saw that the first two runners were from a place called Penn State College and decided that if that was where these two runners were who beat him, then that was where he should be.

So he left and went to Penn State and coached track and became a professor of Olympic sport history. He is a distinguished VIP of almost every Olympic Games in the latter half of the twentieth century, but he never toed the line of an Olympic race. Yet, he has run his 1500-meter Olympic run in every Olympic stadium—climbing over fences, persuading guards—since 1955. And *that* is the spirit of an Olympian—the indomitable spirit that I am trying to write about in this text. There is a drive, greater than normal ambition, that flows from the well of sports.

I remember another story of heroism, the story of a coach and a maintenance man, the man who was responsible for cutting the ice rink out on the lake, as was done all over New England before indoor rinks became the norm, sawing actually, with a tractor pulling a blade that ripped the linear dimension of the rink, scoring it out of the surface of the pond, so that it was essentially a free iceberg within the lake and the cracks and heavings originating from the instabilities on the shore would not affect the oval rink: the ice wound a protective riff.

He was doing this job one day when the tractor he was riding broke through the black pond ice. The ten- and twelve-year-old-boys with hockey sticks in hand, waiting, had watched and stood unmoving as the maintenance man went along the outside edge. Then, like a slow-motion picture, there was a crash and he went down through the surface with the running tractor whose wheel had jammed in the crack. His pant leg caught in the machinery, its engine still sputtering.

Ice closed over the hole, his cries silenced. The coach, the father of one of the boys—a quiet, undramatic man in the boys' eyes—quickly moved out from among them and without hesitation dove through the slush, the cold, the wind and, he too, was gone for a second, a long second. The boys began a silent move toward the hole, vigilant, waiting to grab a coat, a hand, anything, when through the black water, gasping and thrashing, clinging for a hold, the two men came up and were alive! Twenty pairs of mittened hands grabbed and pulled at the one man heaving the other! And the two men passed through them and walked away like gods.

"Walked away like gods." That stuck with me, because I believe that our souls can, at times extend beyond our bodies and drive us to heroic feats, healings and athletic accomplishments. The energy of our body *and* soul coupled together is largely untapped by many people, I think, whereas an athlete taps into the soul every time he or she reaches those levels of the body where the boundaries of the body are met and what is beyond the boundary can only be journeyed into and achieved by the impetus of the soul. What is beyond the boundary of the perceived self is what draws us to athletes. They become a bridge for us, from our world to the metaphysical world. They take us to the gods, and we walk among the gods through them. This vicarious relationship fills stadiums every weekend—as our inner athlete seeks to understand, to better learn, the communion of body and soul.

To strive to push one's body in a channeled effort, while seeking to dive into the recesses of the soul for fortitude, courage, strength is a difficult place for humans to put themselves into. Calling upon grace, strength, is one thing—becoming that grace and strength is something greater still. When we are sacrificing, offering *ourselves* for the greater good, the outcome, the finish line—we have broken the barrier of fear, gone through the limit of self and embody creaturehood, gratitude and humility.

This is when champions become heroes. We all have them, some may not look very athletic at all as they age.

But the heart within them is tangible and infectious. It makes us seek them out so we can be around it.

CHAPTER SIX

A Sense of Balance

Running with the torch was truly an out-of-body experience, a spiritual type of experience. The torch was a very heavy three and one half pounds, and running with it should have been a challenge, but it felt like a feather in my hand. As I ran the kilometer over the infamous Mount Taigetos in the Peloponissos of Greece, I couldn't help but ask, was my Guardian Angel helping me with the weight? Why was I so lucky to run with the torch? It brought to life exactly what the term Olympian means: harmony of body, mind, and spirit.

—Elizabeth Hanley, Olympic Torch runner

WHAT I LOVE ABOUT Betz Hanley's experience is her thinking that her guardian angel helped her with the torch. I think this is a powerful image because the underlying fear in all of us is that we might falter. As humans we are capable of faltering—in stride, in strength.

And then what of the torch? It was symbolic of the greatest athletic realm on earth. It deserved to be held high, held strongly, proudly. What if it dipped? Or fell? We are all carrying something precious over mountain roads and rely in part on faith that an angel is with us and will guide us.

Hanley's story reminds me of the symbolic character "Much-Afraid" in Hannah Hurnard's classic *Hinds' Feet on High Places*. I always related to "Much-Afraid." I have spent the better part of my life in fear. Since my accident some twenty years ago, I have lived every day in fear of the pain that I know can rise in my body without provocation. Stumbling on mountain roads and hoping an angel is there to catch me is an image I can hold close.

This journey we are on has been mainly about the perfection of an athlete's body and soul. The path so far has been flat with sunny days and blue skies—but now we begin to climb. The air will get thinner, the road more difficult, but the reward greater for it.

There is not an athlete I know who has not suffered or undergone pain or injury while training. What one does with injury, how one perceives the struggle, can form a new dimension in personal experience. Great athletic performances are fleeting. Most last only a few minutes or seconds. Fame slowly passes. Aging, injury, pain are part of the journey and can teach us a great deal.

Long years of strenuous physical training encompasses your mind, your guts, till every sinew of your being cries for you to stop pushing it to the limit—yet if you are an elite athlete training for a championship, you cannot listen, you must *will* yourself to *not* listen to yourself, which is an intriguing paradox. And of course that inner voice, or "inner athlete" usually knows where the real limit is—rarely do athletes voluntarily destroy themselves in a race or a competition, which is not to say that they cannot be destroyed, or haven't been or won't be by illegal drugs, bad or careless coaching, mistakes of any kind, but I believe these are the exceptions, not the fare of the thousands of athletes out there jogging an extra two blocks one morning because they feel so strong and just have to do it, or a young skateboarder adding one more heel flip to the routine.

In my years of having to go to the hospital three times a week for physical therapy and for over 160 nerve blocks in my neck and spine to dull the pain in my right arm, shoulder and face to help me regain the full range of motion that was lost during the three months I was initially paralyzed, I found myself escaping, into the caverns of my mind and spirit, to places and days long past, where my body was working again.

I'd slip into the MRI tube and at the same time slip into my ski boots and charge, figuratively down Big Boulder mountain, counting the moguls, bouncing the compression and using the forces of height and depression, quality of snow and light, temperature—to make a perfect run—without falling, or catching an edge. Or I was running my cross-country course—out there amidst farms along mountain roads—anywhere but in the hospital. And before I knew it, the technician on the machine would tell me, "Great! All done. Your doctor will see you this afternoon with the results."

I didn't do this mental exercise by chance; I did it by design and by habit, training. It was in that Thanksgiving Day run, down the bleak November Street of my hometown, surrounded by screaming friends, like Beth and Pam, and well wishers, that I discovered an incredible tool within me. And to this day I claim no credit for its inception, though I believe long hours of training formed the boundaries of its making, and I would have to say that I would be a fool and remiss in my stewardship if I didn't call upon it when needed. The gift is a combination of mental discipline and an ability—a path discovered—that leads to an interior place—the well within that I refer to so often in this text.

Becky Brattain of the U.S. Junior Olympic rifle team relates her experience of this communion,

> As a competitive shooter, I have gained
> the insight to better correlate the con-
> cepts of mind, body and soul. Shooting,
> as are many elements of life, is 90 percent
> mental.

It's not the other competitors, nature's elements, or the shooting environment that affects me. It's not my reactions to those situations, but rather the actions I take. No matter what the situation is, I still must take one shot at a time. Each one counts, time keeps ticking away, and I cannot go back.

These situations have led me to view life in the same manner. Every moment moves on, and every action counts, so every time I make a decision, it must be carefully articulated to ensure that it is the best one I can make. The skills essential in shooting are equally significant in the everyday world. Concentration, relaxation and the ability to focus inwardly are all refined through the sport. Every time I step up to the firing line I am reminded of my driving quote: "If it is to be, it's up to me." No one else can pull the trigger for me and there is no one else to blame for a less than desirable performance. I close my eyes and envision the perfect sight picture, the perfect shot, and the perfect result…a center shot.

It is this type of mental imagery that has trained my mind to dominate my body. I know I can perform, I've done it in the past many times and therefore I know I can do it again, and again. There's no room in my mind during a match for negative thoughts. Unlike that certain little train, I don't think I can, I know it. Each shot is a new match, a new challenge for me to conquer. I compete against myself for my own personal best each time. I aim for performance, not necessarily for score. I cannot control the scores of other competitors, but I can direct my own achievement.

I have repeated the shot process innumerable times in the past eleven years both physically and mentally. Through this repetition I have trained my body to perform almost subconsciously. I have branded upon my mind the way a perfect shot looks and feels. I cannot begin to recount the number of times I have taken a shot without consciously pulling the trigger. I go through the motions. I relax, settle into position, and focus on the target. It is then that my mind takes over. Without consciously making the move, my mind initiates the shot when it is there. It has almost startled me many times when my inner core takes over, but I know that when this occurs, the shot will always be center. My mind has been trained not only to shoot for center, but also to facilitate the conditions *for* a steady shot. A match can be a nervous experience and often my heart rate skyrockets with the pressure. However, as soon as I get into position and begin my routine, it becomes mind over body. Through training, I have acquired the ability to slow my heart rate to the point where I can relax and take a good shot. The mental aspect of the sport, and the inner work required to hone the self to tap into that core, is most challenging, but once conquered, it is the greatest asset of any athlete.

No one but me controls my next move and the only roadblock to success is my own fears. Each time I step up to shoot I set a goal, and each and every time I aim to reach it. It is not something I merely try to attain, but rather something I aggressively attack. I constantly remind myself, "do or do not, there is no try."

These types of experiences are great. They are life's building blocks. How then do we carry them out of the sporting venue into real life, the everyday world? One saying that I have my athletes cut out and paste on their wall is: "Image what you win, win what you image." Imagining what you want—envisioning it—seeing it out there is a very powerful mental tool. Mental imaging is a great sports training tool. It has been used by divers and gymnasts for years—it rehearses the neuromuscular pathways with the movement you are seeing yourself go through. It sets a pattern inside your muscles and nerves that mimics the action when you do it for real. In a way, "walking through" the process in your mind is like a light practice inside your being. You have set the foundation for a perfect shot—a successful race. We can carry this into our everyday life and apply the same principles—see what it is you want to win out there and then pursue it.

Visualization is just one great tool sports give us.

Appreciating and interiorizing values are others. Because this idea of body and soul, if it means anything at all worth talking about, certainly must transcend mere superficiality—mere "feeling good"—to stick with us and have meaning. It must be more than just a runner's high or the exhilaration of a "good game." Its imprint must carry us to another level of existence to have lasting meaningful value.

I think one of the greatest tools I have been given in life is to use what I learned and felt when I was well, to carry me through the rough times when I felt despair or was injured. I have used stories and examples of visualization techniques, mental discipline, sheer toughness to show how the rigorous nature of sport can toughen and solidify the connection between body and soul so that when we are tested to the utmost, either in a test of character or health or both, we can meet the challenge with dignity. The loss of bodily function or skill or the diminishment of mental capacity is a terrifying thing for the person experiencing it and for the caretakers and family and friends witnessing it.

But it is the inevitable outcome of our very existence to experience sickness and eventual death. Lifetime sports can be a great asset to help us gradually work through aging while still experiencing the rigors of competition. Rowing, bowling and running are just a few examples of sports that can carry one through the declining years with dignity and grace. Nothing perks up the respect for another competitor more than when you are passed by someone who is clearly older than you are and is still competing well! I remember a great T-shirt slogan, "Age and trickery will always overcome youth and skill." I saw this T-shirt on a competitive rower at the World Master's rowing championships as he was pulling his single up from the water and balancing it on his bald, wrinkled and suntanned eighty-year-old head. I just had to laugh and go over and talk to him.

He had been a competitive rower since college, sixty years earlier. He said that slicing lines on still water with his hull through early morning mists was his daily prayer. In his union of hands on the oars, hull gliding over the water and fresh damp air cooling his lungs and clearing his mind, he recognized he was fragile as was his boat, yet strong and true so long as he stayed the course and didn't wander.

It is a beautiful image and perhaps that is why I am attracted to the sport of rowing. One can go fast or slow, one must stay in balance, one must stay within the buoys—stay the course—one must pull and push as hard as you can to approach swing and near flight. One can paddle effortlessly in gratitude and appreciation in the hushed morning silhouette between sun and land. In rowing one can remove the trappings of the body—no pads, no helmets, no cleats, no other competitor needed even, to enjoy, to play like a child with a boat before the Creator and in the Creator. Rowing is a love affair with earth and water, body and soul, God and creature. Silence is broken only by the sound of the effort—telltale wheels rolling along the slide, the *ssshhhhh* of the hull through the water surface, the mute plop of rhythmic oars. Balance, timing—body and soul I knew what the old man meant when he said "it was his daily prayer"—he meant it was all the prayer he needed because it was enough, it fulfilled and satisfied the body *and* the soul's need to be one, to rejoin, to return to the place of its making. And rowing is very womblike, insular.

To return to the Creator is the ultimate end of the journey for the experience of body and soul. And so we have arrived at the door of a mountain hut, high up in the thin layers of rarified air, musing over the essence of ourselves and the role that sport plays in our existence. Body and soul equal, body and soul reaching, palms up, touching the door pushing it gently open to enter, to merge. If one balances the body and soul experience a greater union is achieved, a greater awareness risen to. This awareness, this point of elevation is the goal, the pin-point precision of mirroring our image with that of the gods, and we should seek it, grasp it and make it our own, with our own stamp and signature—for our body and soul experience is unique. Our creaturehood culminates in its return to the emulsion with the Creator, ultimate harmony and unity, one body one soul, many bodies and many souls no longer.

The frailty of the human condition defines body. We can touch it, see it; we are one with it and, we are it. The ethereal nature of the soul is the sanctifying element of bread and wine turned body and blood. Something acts as catalyst and transformation occurs.

I remember once taking quite a sizeable detour on a trip in order to return to a favorite place of prayer—and finding it under construction. The small chapel felt cold and in the opaque light seemed without life. The Eucharist was not in the tabernacle and the candles were unlit. Outside a construction crew was changing walls, ceilings, adding walkways. It seemed as if even the spiritual was in a state of flux. But God was there. It was the same feeling one gets at San Damiano in Assisi—that the very rocks themselves could start to sing, they are so permeated with holiness. The sanctity of the *place* weighs heavy in the air.

The juxtaposition of the bustling world outside and the

soul trying to be still and to be at peace within is symbolic of life—of our trying to bring forth order and sense, beauty and balance in a world under construction.

CHAPTER SEVEN

Living in The Resurrection

In the battle of life it is not the critic that counts…the credit belongs to the man who is actually in the arena; whose face is marred by dust and sweat and blood…who at the best knows in the end triumph of high achievements; and who at the worst, if he fails, at least fails while daring greatly, so that his place shall never be with those cold and timid souls who have tasted neither victory or defeat.

—Theodore Roosevelt

I THINK THE GREAT MOMENTS of heroism in sport happen when the soul reaches up from its latent state and joins the body in motion, voice, deed. Perhaps that is why, at such moments of physical or personal breakthrough—people finally notice, the act is finally done. It is like a transcendence has happened. Something has changed, it is tangible and it comes after trials and great sacrifice.

The importance of the resurrection is a key understanding to an athlete's approach to life and to the world. If there is any one way to understand an athlete's mind and drive that you can make your own—it is that an athlete always strives to live in the resurrection.

The trilogy of judgment (competition), crucifixion (ultimate win/lose situation) and resurrection (back in to practice and training again, over and over, season after season) is the basic rhythm of an athlete's approach to life, to a season, to a career, to a game.

The impetus to desire to place one's performance on public display for better or for worse is the nature of competitive sport—and some games and play. The fact that all cultures play games, to me as a Christian, is logical! It tells me that the very nature of God is universal. The smallest remnant of "what play is" that tiny quantum theory particle, that smallest seed that is still seed, that is play—that is what sparks, promotes, drives our joy of God. God is the essence of joy. And we seek joy in play. We seek escape from the everyday world, just as we seek a quiet small chapel, to be in the world, yet removed and sheltered from it. There are rules here—respect, quiet, removing one's hat—just as certain as the governing of the rules of chess.

So when athletes speak of running or lifting as being spiritual, this is not so far out and far-fetched as it seems.

And so to seek to emulate athletics' good values: to compete, to risk judgment, to praise, to resurrect oneself or a team at large and then, no matter which is the outcome, begin anew the next day again and again, is a magnetic dynamic, a force, a cultural mover. And so sport is huge. Its impact universal, its allure primal—we relate to it unconsciously because our ancestors have participated in it in our families, communities, churches, countries, tribes for thousands of years.

Take away the soul and sport is flat, without passion—there is no crucifixion as there is no need for a resurrection. Yet, I already hear people chiding—but what about sport that is without competition? For health alone? For the fun of it? It is my opinion and has always been that without some skill there is no fun. If you can't jump rope, you don't want to jump and you don't jump rope. So there is always competition even if it is only between a rope and a human, a human's first jump and the hundredth—a child's first kick of a ball and the dichotomy of ball and self and getting to the ball on the rug even before kicking. There are so many obstacles that compete with us as we try to run "the good race" even if we seek to not be competitive with others.

Body and soul have a constant and everlasting relationship. Even as in Christ in death, it seeks, it waits, to rise. I think it is the rising that is the unconscious identity perhaps of people—to sport and to athletes—they see something of God. And they want it. The good side of that equation gives hope, joy, peace, well-being; the hard side runs amuck in sports' manmade media frenzies that we see in some megalomaniac sports figures. Balance is the key.

Perhaps that is why of all the sports, balance sports hold the crowd in a hush of wonder. In football, running, soccer—crowds stand and cheer! Head-on human contact is brute and courageous and primitive. But balance? Balance is mysterious, ethereal, it can be dangerous, it can overcome the body in space. The body can fall, wobble; balance beams, dive platforms, these are all external symbols of the inner self metaphorically wanting, yearning to cross from point to point. Balance is a primal key and signal in the brain and body for safety. Its execution makes us hush, *ohhhhh* and *ahhhh*. Why?

Because the mortal question is in jeopardy—death or resurrection? Salvation or fall? These are metaphors for questions we all ask. Will I make it—to heaven—or will I fall? Eat the fruit or don't eat it. These are the quantum particles of faith that we can see in the balance and that we desire to be all right—walked across, held on to without falling. The connection of body and soul is unique, primal, and integral to life. Resurrection without death is impossible. Balance is the space the split-second between words, within the action.

I had a friend who passed away, a Greek woman named Helen. She said that when she prayed she never asked God for anything; she only prayed to be protected from those split seconds, those instances when disaster might hit—where life can be changed forever. She called them by the Greek word *stigmi*. Helen had a dignity about her. She was not educated, coming as she did from a village in Greece, but her training was from the ancient gymnasium of dance, music, painting, sculpture and physical education. She read ancient Greek and Greek poetry. During World War II, she was interned and sentenced to death. Moments before her execution was to take place, she was freed because one of her captors recognized her as the daughter of a physician who had saved a friend's life once. During the war she saw her father and two brothers executed. She came to see the world as a series of fateful moments.

For Helen, balance in life was achieved from her background, but it was maintained in her understanding of how the universe worked, that there were these moments, *stigmi*, that could alter your world forever. For Helen the balance of life was the intersections of the *stigmi*—either life was kept in balance, or it was irreversibly thrown out of kilter if balance was lost for an instant. Some might think of these occurrences as fate, but Helen didn't accept that. Fate is not preventable, it is something that happens no matter what, and she felt that you could alter the *stigmi* by praying about them, healing them and, in a very proactive stance, preventing them.

Hers was an interesting approach to daily life. I think many athletes prepare expressly to avoid the *stigmi*. Avoid the hole on the road that can trip you and ruin a career. Avoid the irregular grip on a high bar that can send you to the floor and out of the competition. Avoid the charging wide receiver determined to attack and interrupt your reception. Athletes live at the edge of the *stigmi* all the time. They must learn to be comfortable there—another strength that I believe draws people to seek athletic training. They see the value in conditioning and practicing balance by knowing and exploring the edges of their abilities.

You can close your eyes and imagine with me the gymnast or diver that daily trains in the realms of physical balance. How does that train the mind? Wouldn't it equally train the soul? Athletes train within those realms every day, and that is very special indeed.

Moreover, once athletes have stretched themselves to those edges, they become, to an extent, "larger than life." In the face of nagging injuries or stories of severe accidents in *other* gyms or on *other* teams, athletes train on. Athletes can't focus on those issues or they would never stretch themselves forward. Injury is taken in hand.

Athletes tend to visualize and fantasize the world as perfect and in their control. That is a positive training tool. However, when fate steps in and waves its hand and something like cancer, or heart attack or car accident happens, athletes too are forced to complete the equations of what life is all about.

As a coach, I feel I contribute to this universal prayer of self-realization by being privileged to teach from the background of knowing pain. It reminds me daily, and serves as my taskmaster, to acknowledge and live my creaturehood, my mortality. It is only by humbly knowing this, that we can ever truly worship God. For me, to elevate sport to a sacred place where one can go and use visualization techniques while getting another MRI or while lying in yet another operating room, is grace. And to see the beauty of the human form executing balance at the level of completeness and complexity for which it was created is prayer and worship. To use the tools and techniques of sport and training to overcome the hurdles of life, to transcend, is the greatest gift a coach can give or an athlete can learn.

CHAPTER EIGHT

Breakthrough Kinesis

"…Only the sublime is worthwhile, everything else is held up to it."
—from *Philosophy in the Bleachers,* George Santayana

WHEN A BREAKTHROUGH takes place, when an athlete accomplishes the heroic act, others are somehow emboldened and enabled. There is a rebirth of hope. The hero soon has company.

I have been lucky, what could have been a career-ending accident led me to greater athletic heights, as a competitor and as a coach. The transition from the athlete to the coach is not necessarily easy. I remember the first time I tried to step out of the role of an athlete—at this point a basketball player, since I had captained my basketball team in high school—when I was asked to referee a basketball game to get my officiating license. Sounds easy enough. If you play the game well you should be able to officiate, right? Well, the transition wasn't that easy for me. I followed the game well enough, the action, but I kept waiting for someone to throw me the ball! I was thinking on only one level. In time I might have been able to train myself out of the athlete role and into the official's role, but I was frustrated at looking like a goofy official when I was a pretty good basketball player. The roles seemed confusing to me and I didn't like being on a court and not feeling entirely in control of myself.

In my injury some of the necessary mind-set changes that needed to be made from active athlete to coach were forced upon me from the long period of inactivity. All sport became a more interior process. I think I might have been a good basketball referee at that time too, but that opportunity was not before me. What was afforded me was the opportunity to coach crew. I would lie in bed at night, the anxiety over pain and my future steadily being replaced now by images of long artful oars, sun-drenched rowers, silky smooth water cut through temporarily by the bow of a rowing shell. I'd lie awake at night, restless and usually hurting from my neck and back and found I could engulf my thoughts, transport myself, to the situation I was confronted with in crew. Did I have the right line-up of oarsmen? Were the women getting enough water time? Is the rigging right? Can I tweak it just a bit more to get an inch out of the strokes? (One inch per stoke with over 200 strokes in 2,000 meters is a substantial margin.)

I had one very good men's four that was powerful enough that I could adjust the rigging (the mechanical adjustments of a rowing shell that affect the forces generated by the crew) week by week, and their strength and athletic ability would add to the adjustment just the prescribed increase of speed and responsiveness.

I adjusted the boat without telling them and they performed at a higher level—finally winning a national medal. It sounds simple. But one must almost be able to sense—and I use the word *sense* because you are in fact *not* in the boat with the rowers and you *can't* feel the pressure changes in the hands and feet that they feel so you must be astute enough to pick up on the subtleties and process the outcome quickly and accurately. Human performance is a great variable in and of itself. It isn't a machine or a computer. It is fluid not static. In my case I think I see the nuances of stroke mechanics because of all the nights I lay awake using the images of motion—like rowing—to act within. Since I couldn't move as such, I was vicariously using their motion. I was inside their motion.

I was, night after night, day after day, imaginatively becoming part of what they were doing; this enabled me to be a much better coach in the launch. I gained an intuitive sense of their level of exhaustion, skill, ability and potential. I seemed to be able to size up other crews' interior nature just by watching them walk on the dock or by their first oar-plant. I could warn my crews which crews might give them more trouble than their record might seem.

As I said earlier, part of this was from my years as a Fine Arts major, looking at paintings, and painting with oils and watercolors. My eye was trained already, but my accident trained the space between my vision and my speech. I could communicate what I was intuitively sensing in a crew to help them.

Again, this all sounds easy but I have seen coaches look and look and never see the problem the crew is doing right in front of them or they can't articulate what it is that is wrong. I believe that by being driven inward, I resurfaced as a better coach because I had to hone my vision and perception. I couldn't jump in the boat and row with them: I wasn't able to do that, but I could help them through my own interior journey.

I always try to draw the athlete from the present experience into the greater meaning—the bigger picture. I think it is part of a coach's job to draw the parallels of the game, or the skill, or the competition to the larger life lessons. It is a service to an athlete with a temper, to teach him or her that aggression and determination is good—so long as it doesn't get out of hand, and it stays between the lines on the court. Once the game is over, the aggression gets put away until the next game.

It is a difficult time to be a coach. Today's society is more litigious than a generation ago, and some are not appreciative of the time and skill afforded them by a dedicated coach. I hope I don't sound too old or old-fashioned, but there was a time when a coach was like a teacher or other professional—and when the coach said something, it meant that it got done without question or remark—but these realms seem fuzzier today. Athletes, and parents of athletes, and conferences question more today and—one need only glance at the NCAA rulebook to see this—perhaps rightfully so. Sports and the money in sports and the opportunities in professional sports and big-time college athletics can certainly turn your head. The abuses within "the system," within coaching staffs, within conferences are no secret. Locker rooms are full of stories. But the stories of the good coaches, the stories of the good assistant coaches who work hard and try to act morally and fair, don't hit the headlines.

For me, the best part of myself is being a rowing coach. The greatest thing for me to hear or see is a phone call or E-mail that starts with, "Hey Coach…"

I feel proud of those at the other end and I feel proud of myself for trying to help and share as best I could and having it work. Perhaps it was partly fate. Michael Novak, in *The Joy of Sports* talks about philosophy and about the hand fate plays in sport. He looks at sport more as an observer than a participant, but his observations are credible and profound. As a coach, I have found his perceptions of the athlete's performance to be right on and experientially important. He looks at sport, not as a rulebook of regulation, or possible lawsuits; he looks at the beauty of sport and performance and the movement of the human form at the moments of its highest achievements. He distills the power of athletic experience as the revelatory moments of perfect form. Novak looks at these psychically enhanced performances, if you will, in sport and likens them to being or coming from or belonging to another plane (the spiritual, perhaps, in Novak's understanding).

But Novak also captures the essence of what I call a "breakthrough kinesis" (for a full description of this idea, please see "Quest: The National Journal for Physical Education," 2003) in the following passage:

Tens of thousands of passes are thrown every year, thousands of games are played in grammar schools, high schools, colleges, and professional stadia; all the routines are thoroughly known. Occasionally, however, often enough to stir the heart, a player or a team executes a play so beautifully, achieves such classic perfection, that it is as though they cease for a moment to be pedestrian and leap into a realm of precision as lovely as a statue of Praxiteles. Athletic achievement, like the achievements of the heroes and the gods of Greece, is the momentary attainment of perfect form—as though there were, hidden away from mortal eyes, a perfect way to execute a play, and suddenly a player or a team has found it and sneaked a demonstration down to earth. A great play is a revelation. The curtains of ordinary life part, and perfection flashes for an instant before the eye.

The phrase "hidden away from mortal eyes, a perfect way" is the key to Novak's explanation. Where is the "perfect way" "hidden," yet available to the extent that we witness it enough times that people recognize it, philosophers think about it, writers elaborate on it and athletes occasionally achieve it? Does it lie in the realm of what I am trying to touch upon and give us food for thought? I hope so. I believe so.

I think one must answer that it lies within the mind/body experience in those rare yet certain intersections of space, planes, consciousness, movement and moment. The element of "moment" or "timing" is unique to breakthrough because it places the action in a unique reference to all other actions past and future. A breakthrough kinesis is an incident when a performance barrier is broken and the human performance suddenly jumps to another height— seemingly defying science and entering the realm of the mystical.

Most athletes and coaches would agree that we advance physiologically by plateaus. We reach plateaus, we stay there awhile and then we advance, upward to the next level, the next plateau. The training curve is rarely a straight line or a symmetrical curve; rather, it looks more like steps. A "breakthrough kinesis"—that is to say a breakthrough in performance—is such an advancement. The unconscious moves the mind/body to another level in a leap forward where it remains for a time before another breakthrough. This leap is in the realm of the intangible that stumps science because it cannot be reduced to any "thing." It has, is, and forever retains, the element of the mythical.

And, I speculate, that the collective unconscious explored by the eminent Swiss psychologist Carl Jung helps to explain the mythical. For if we do carry within ourselves a collective memory of the experiences from all those who have lived before us to the very beginnings of our origins, we carry, and in fact *are* those origins, extending presumably, to times in human experience akin to the essence of the mythical exchange in Michelangelo's fresco of the creation of Adam in the Sistine Chapel, the energy of God creating. That exchange between God and Adam symbolically includes all the time and space between Creator and human experience—a space that our present self at times taps into and integrates into a current-day occurrence.

One example of an athlete tapping into sources within that are sometimes nameable, and sometimes unnamable and unknown to them, is the swimmer Erin Phenix, Olympic gold medalist in the 400-meter freestyle relay—someone who spends a good deal of time submersed, quite literally in an insular, interior environment. Erin was not a star out of high school, swimming with the

Cincinnati Marlins. But she got to swim at the University of Texas in Austin where her coach (an Olympic medalist herself) told her, "I want you to know you have a chance to be an Olympian." This meant everything to Erin. And her lifelong dream to become something great started to take shape.

Seeded fifty-eighth at the Olympic trials, where they only take the top six to be on the team, she remembers that she "just knew" she was going to make it. She wasn't nervous, she just went out, enjoyed the swimming, confident that she was going to be an Olympian. When the cut was down to the top eight at the semifinals, she was eighth. She had dropped three seconds off her best time ever, which was light years in swimming. And in the finals, when only the top six get to wear an Olympic uniform, she was sixth. Her dream to make the team had been realized through the impetus of a good coach, her own talent, fate, and her creed that, "anything is possible with faith." Her dream to win another gold goes on—through the throes of mono and long grueling hours in the pool she swims.

Erin Phenix entered that mythical realm of being some-one's hero. It is a great responsibility as well as a great honor. As I said earlier, I have told my rowers that what makes someone great is when, twenty-five years after their last medal, they walk down the banks of a regatta, or on the deck of a pool, and people come up and say hello and chat, and find you approachable, because you are a good person as well as a good athlete. And the great ones do stick out in a crowd. So many worn out words produce adages of how victory is fleeting—I won't reuse any of them, since they have been said much more eloquently than I can hope to write—but I will say that I believe it is true.

Greatness always involves giving away to someone or something else—time, hours, training, sacrifice; all spent for a higher cause. It is cyclical at its best and falls flat when it is self-serving. Greatness of the inner self, the soul is everlasting. It never wears thin and it is always recognizable. It is every coach's dream to aspire to it, or to say something to their athletes that spurs them to aspire to it. Fate and greatness choose their own.

Afterword

I have had many wonderful crews in my twenty years of coaching. Some won medals, some did not. Some won national championships, some just participated and gave it their all. And I loved every minute of it. I always try to be at the dock when they launch and when they return because, for me, the real race isn't just at the finish line. The real result is in the human product that is generated through the hours and days; the years of training—that go into the minutes of racing glory or despair.

Although I could say to my crew as they push off the dock, "Go get 'em! Kick some butts out there," my final words to the crew at large are usually, "Have fun."

And I believe that. I believe that training must be invigorating and fun in order for people to succeed. And that fun doesn't mean there are days of lollygagging and goofing around, or we don't care what happens win or lose we want to have fun—quite the opposite. I think the fun that I try to instill is the idea of pursuing excellence, as I have indicated earlier—the pursuit of *arête* is the fun of sport. Our goal is the betterment of skill and self; let the medals fall where they may.

I've had many successful crews suffer angst while trying to pass through the trials of self-discovery as they proceeded toward their goal. And that always bothered me inside—that I might somehow fail them as a coach who was also someone trying to elevate their experience of sport, not simply elevate their skill.

And it is hard, as a woman coach in particular. You are a woman in a man's world. A strong, confident man is called "capable" and "someone not to be fooled with." But a strong, confident woman is sometimes dismissed with a less complimentary term.

I have sat and talked with my women athletes who were new to competition and new to going into the depths of themselves to find and bring out that inner drive and determination. Some women are just so shy about exerting, sweating, gaining muscle mass and competence that it really becomes an emotional issue in the way of their physical performance. They need—not so much of a physical breakthrough, but a personal breakthrough.

I've had some challenging talks with women athletes about being true to their potential, without apologies for a world that might expect something else from them. And the transformation I've seen in them has been wonderful—spiritual. I've seen women gain an inner understanding from sport that they will carry with them in every aspect of their lives. And I haven't hidden this revelation from the guys on the team either. I've had the privilege to coach some extraordinary male crews who epitomized the finest aspects of arête. I encourage everyone to make an interior, philosophical journey of self-discovery and identity through sport.

But one of the greatest examples I can give to bring the philosophical nature of this book into concrete reality is the story of two women rowers I coached who *became* "body and soul." It happened one day at practice.

It was a dreary day, misty and cool. Rain had just dropped, and the mountain lake reflected an ink-black surface. The lake was unusually smooth and still. There were no ripples on the water. There was no wind to mar its surface. The trees had not yet started to show leaves. The day seemed bare and stark.

When these two women showed up to practice, they asked if they might go home instead since it was such a miserable day. I told them they could leave if they wanted—but I reminded them that this was the last time they would ever row their boat as college rowers, the night before leaving for the national championships. They would never do this again—but they could leave if they wanted.

They chose to stay. I was so proud of them! We did our usual pre-race rehearsal of going over every square foot of the race plan, so there were no surprises, no room for error. My launch was close to their boat and our figures reflected perfectly on the water's surface like a mirror.

When we completed our work, I shut the engine off and both boats—racing shell and coaching launch—drifted to a stop. I thanked them for being athletes. I thanked them for being there every day, day after day. I reminded them to look around one last time—out here on the lake, away from the land—to soak in the day, the moment, the work, the effort, the preparation. I told them to make a place in their soul for this moment, to have for the years to come—for that "someday" when life comes around and bites them, and they need a place of wonderment to escape to. I told them they can always come here. To carry this place inside them because it was theirs. They earned it. They deserved it. They looked at me and understood. Their eyes said everything.

When I drove my launch away, I was symbolically separating my four years of effort that were spent helping to mold them as athletes. The years of worrying about them, hoping that they would perform as well as I knew they could. I was making the separation between all the practices and the preparation to actually start for the nationals the next day. This day was like no other. It would never return again—but right now it was ours.

As the distance increased between us. The lake seemed to become a cathedral of mountain and weather. It seemed sacred. When I looked back at them, they had lain down in the boat. They were no longer sitting up like rowers, competitors, trained with knowledge and talent. They were laying down across the cockpit of the rowing shell, in-line with the boat, oars resting perpendicular reflecting on the water. That was when I knew—they were *inside* the boat. By lowering themselves, and resting within the gunnels, they became one with the experience of the rowing shell, the sky, the water, the moment.

They had their hands resting so lightly on the oars, it seemed to me the perfect grip—the one that I had so often tried to get them to do—to "lighten up," to "feel the water on the oar," "through the oar—not to dig the oar in," to "move the boat past the oar-plant and not just push the water past the boat."

They had the perfect grip. They were inside the rowing.

It was especially poignant to me, two days later, when this crew took third at the nationals. Another crew from our team had won another event—which was great. But these two rowers in the pair had worked for years, every day, through injury, disappointment, pain, and would emerge as champions, too. They were the epitome of the trainable athletes who tried to embody every suggestion, every image.

And when I peered through the fog that day at the Dad Vail National Championships, I saw a dot in the middle lane come under the bridge in first, another dot come under bridge in second—and I held my breath and I remember saying "please God, please," and they were there. Those two women were the third dot under the bridge. They had done it! Fourth, fifth and sixth were safely tucked behind them. I knew, and I sensed that they knew also, that they were going to grab a medal. I had always told all my crews that any color medal is a good color medal. And they had bronze.

It was the perfect ending to their collegiate rowing careers. These two athletes *became* what they found on the lake that last day of practice. They became the strength and the mystery of their "boat prayer." Body and soul had delivered.